THE CREATIVE BOOK OF

Greeting Cards

THE CREATIVE BOOK OF

Greeting Cards

Annette Claxton

a Salamander book

Published by Salamander Books Limited
LONDON • NEW YORK

Published by Salamander Books Ltd.,
129-137 York Way, London N7 9LG, United Kingdom.

©Salamander Books Ltd. 1989

ISBN 0 86101 470 7

Distributed in Canada by Cavendish Books Inc.,
Unit 5, 801 West 1st Street,
North Vancouver, B.C. V7P 1A4.
Phone (604) 985-2969.

CREDITS

Editor: Jo Finnis

Designer: Glynis Edwards

Photographer: Steve Tanner

Artwork: John Hutchinson

Filmset by: The Old Mill, London

Colour origination by: Bantam Litho Ltd., England

Printed in Belgium by: Proost International Book Production

CONTENTS

INTRODUCTION

Hand-made cards are always a delight to receive, show to friends, keep for ever, perhaps framed and on permanent display. They are personalized cards for special people, made with care and affection to mark an occasion or event. A wedding card made from material used to make the bride's or bridesmaids' dresses or a congratulation card specially made to mark a long-awaited examination result will add much pleasure to the event.

The cards in this book cover a wide range of techniques. Some take only a few minutes to make, others a good deal longer. You will be familiar with a number of the methods used, but there are plenty of new ones to try. Step-by-step photographs and accompanying instructions will make the techniques easy to follow and help you to achieve the best results. The templates at the back of the book are actual size for ease of use.

Many of the cards are designed to suit more than one occasion and will give you inspiration to create your own designs. Do experiment and let your imagination work for you to achieve truly creative results.

There are several important points that will help you to achieve hand-made rather than home-made results. The correct weight of card will not curl or fall over, so always use card of at least 200-300 gsm (134-201lb/sq in). If you use a card that is too thick, it will give you as many problems as one that is too thin.

To make a neat fold, score the card on the right side with a light cut using a sharp craft knife and a steel ruler, just piercing the top layer of card. The card will then fold in a straight line. Before you start scoring the fold, look carefully at the main photograph of the card to be sure you understand the measurement given. Unless

otherwise stated, all the cards in this book are folded vertically. Always measure carefully and mark with a hard sharp pencil to create a fine line. Should a card, despite your careful measuring, be crooked, trim a new straight edge using a set-square and with the card folded so that you cut through both back and front thicknesses at once. Draw the blade twice along the cutting edge.

Card comes in a variety of finishes: cloud effect, metallic, parchment style, textured, glossy and matt. Tissue, brown, origami, marbled, wall and wrapping paper, foil and plastic bags have all been used to create different effects and textures.

EQUIPMENT

You will probably already have many of the materials in the photograph opposite and it is not necessary for card-making to become an expensive hobby. However, several of these items are essential for producing professional-looking cards: a steel ruler for measuring and using as a cutting edge; a craft knife with snap-off blades which will ensure you always cut cleanly; a set-square to help you achieve accurate right-angles. We have used a self-healing cutting board with a printed grid, which is most effective, but you can also use thick cardboard as a base for cutting.

Keep a pair of scissors just for cutting paper and card, saving your good scissors for fabric, since paper blunts scissors very quickly. Embroidery scissors are a great help for small pieces of work and tight corners. Pinking shears give an interesting effect when used for edging card, paper or fabric.

ADHESIVES

With practice, spray glue gives a good finish and can also be used on fabric, but care must be taken to stop the glue drifting on to surrounding furnishings (see below). The advantage of spray glue is that paper that has been spray glued can be lifted and re-positioned if necessary. If you make any smudges on the card with the glue, they can usually be removed by gentle rubbing with lighter fuel on a piece of cotton wool. Do make sure that any spray glue or spray paint you use is ozone-friendly.

Spray glue and spray paint should always be used in a 'spray booth'. To make one, set up a large cardboard box on its side, with newspaper in front to protect whatever it is standing on. Place an old magazine or telephone directory inside the box to use as a base for spraying. Lay the card, paper or fabric to be glued face down on the open pages and spray approximately 30cm (12in) away from the surface. When you have finished spraying, turn over a page of the magazine or directory so that you have a clean base again for the next spraying job. When all the pages have been used, simply discard and replace with a new one.

We have also used a rubber-based adhesive. This is useful since any excess can simply be rubbed off the card when the glue has dried. It is not so easily removed from fabric, so use sparingly. Always read and follow the manufacturer's instructions on the tube. A glue pen is also useful when you need to direct a narrow line of glue onto the edge of a card, or onto a narrow piece of ribbon, lace or paper.

Another method of attaching fabric to card is to use a bonding web. The design is drawn onto the smooth side of the bonding material and then ironed onto the wrong side of the fabric. The

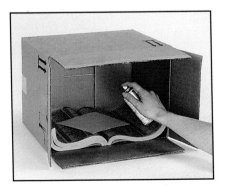

A 'spray booth' should always be used when spraying glue or paint and is very easy to set up using a cardboard box on its side. We have demonstrated steps without using a booth in the book, but this is only to enable you to see what is happening more clearly. Always remember to use 'ozone-friendly' spray glue or paints.

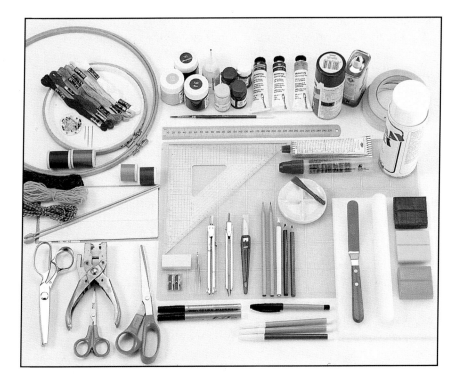

design is then cut out and the paper peeled off to reveal the glue web. The fabric is then ironed direct onto the card with a warm dry iron. Provided the card is not lightweight, ie under 240 gsm (160lb/sq in), it will not curl. This is a useful way to glue on fabric which is prone to fraying, since the bonding web binds the edges with glue. It has been used for several cards in the book.

Double-sided adhesive tape is invaluable for a professional finish. Cut into strips and place where needed, then remove paper 'backing' to reveal the second adhesive side.

USEFUL ITEMS

A hole punch is useful for making decorative holes, punching out circles from coloured paper to be glued onto a card or for making holes in gift tags, through which ribbon can be threaded and attached to parcels. We have used a pair of dividers as a safe method for making holes in card to sew on buttons, etc. A stout needle could be used instead. Coloured felt-tipped pens are good for adding details to motifs and can be taped onto a compass. Gold and silver pens are effective and are especially useful for writing messages inside black or dark-coloured cards. If you do not have these pens, cut a piece of paper slightly smaller than the card's dimensions and fold down centre. Run a thin line of glue along outside of fold and attach to inside fold of card. Tweezers are highly recommended for holding small items when applying glue.

MODELLING MATERIAL

We have used Fimo modelling material in the book (bottom right-hand corner of photograph). It can be moulded and cut into various shapes, then baked in an oven for a few minutes to harden (please follow manufacturer's instructions) and glued onto card. A small rolling pin and board is useful for rolling out the clay and a palette knife can be used for lifting flat shapes from the board.

SOURCES

Magpie tendencies are a great help when creating cards. You will need small amounts of many different materials, since you will be making one-off items in many cases. Materials for cards can be found everywhere! Doll specialists are invaluable for tiny accessories; stationers will yield a whole variety of 'stickers' and transfers, as well as card and paper; and craft shops have all sorts of suitable items. Also, it is useful to trawl the shelves of supermarkets, toy and home-ware shops, looking with a fresh and imaginative eye to see how items could be used 'differently'.

Inspiration can come from other sources, too. Have a look through books on patchwork, quilting, embroidery, knitting and other crafts, as well as children's books, to find design ideas which could be adapted to making original cards. Other sources of designs or motifs include magazines, travel brochures, seed catalogues, old greeting cards, postcards, exhibitions, museums, shop windows, haberdashery departments, cocktail, button and bead shops. A single, unusual button could provide a theme for a whole card design. Second-hand and charity shops can be an inexpensive source of old bead necklaces and lace.

WHAT TO BUY

Packets of sequin 'sweepings' consist of a mixture of many different shapes and colours and are invaluable for decoration. Sequin waste is an inexpensive, effective and versatile material. As already mentioned, buttons come in a variety of delightful designs and are very cheap to buy. The shank can be cut off, so that the buttons lie flat, if necessary. Christmas fabrics can often be bought in squares known as fat quarters, as can felt in jewel colours.

Ribbon is a vital element and is available in a great many widths and colours. There are also attractive floral, tartan and printed theme ribbons. From satin to gift-wrap ribbon, it will all curl over scissors, as will paper cut into narrow strips. It can also be woven, plaited and glued. Braid is another very useful material and again is available in a variety of forms and colours. Flowers are ever-popular motifs, and you can achieve quite different effects by using different sorts — dried flowers (see Petal Valentine, page 60), ribbon flowers (Wedding Bouquet, page 78), golden roses and leaves (50 Golden Years of Marriage, page 81) and fabric flowers (Easter Bonnet, page 62). Paper doilies come in a whole range of sizes and patterns and can be used in various ways — see New Year Dove, page 56; Petal Valentine, page 60.

——MOUNTS AND BLANKS——

The photograph below shows a selection of ready-cut card blanks and mounts. When mounting a piece of work into a window frame, trim to within 6mm (¼in) of the aperture, so that it will not be too bulky. On 3-fold cards, it is a good idea to mark the inside left-hand corner with a cross, to avoid mounting your work upside-down. Mark centre panel with a cross to indicate the top when using the card landscape, again to avoid mounting upside-down. Pencil dots marking the corners of the window on the right side of your work will help you to centre it. If you do make a card the wrong way up, cut off the whole front and re-mount on a new card.

MAKING A 3-FOLD WINDOW CARD

Decide on the size of card you want and multiply width measurement by three. Draw out on to piece of chosen card using a sharp pencil. Mark the fold lines. Any pencil lines can be removed with a soft eraser; do not use pen.

Measure piece of work for mounting and cut a window to fit. Visually, it is more pleasing to leave a wider border at base of card. Score the two fold marks on right side of card with craft knife. Be careful not to cut right through the card. You can use the offcut windows as gift tags.

Looking at the 3-fold card from the inside, cut off a 1mm (¹/₈in) strip from the left side so that it will fit neatly when folded and glued. If you always put a cross on the inside top left-hand corner, you will never mount your work upside-down.

──ENVELOPES AND BOXES──

Once you have decided to make a card, you will need an envelope. Envelopes are not standard sizes, but card mount suppliers (listed on page 120) will hold a good selection. In case you cannot purchase an envelope to fit your card, there are instructions below for making a plain envelope. If you want to make a special envelope, there are instructions opposite on how to make an origami envelope, which can be made from any decorative paper. Some cards are three-dimensional and need a box. These, too, are available from card mount suppliers. Shaped cards will need extra support to protect them. Use card, foam or wadding (batting).

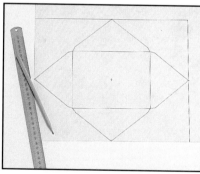

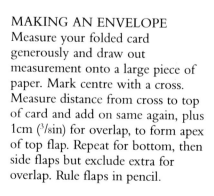

MAKING AN ENVELOPE

Measure your folded card generously and draw out measurement onto a large piece of paper. Mark centre with a cross. Measure distance from cross to top of card and add on same again, plus 1cm (³/₈in) for overlap, to form apex of top flap. Repeat for bottom, then side flaps but exclude extra for overlap. Rule flaps in pencil.

Cut out your envelope, score (if using card) and fold in side flaps. Fold in bottom flap and glue to side flaps using a glue pen. Glue down top flap when you have written your card.

MAKING AN ORIGAMI ENVELOPE

An origami envelope is a novel way to present a card or a gift token. You need an accurate square of any kind of paper. We cut a piece of paper 33cm (13in) square. Take your square, fold a diagonal line across and crease. Fold again in the opposite direction, do not crease but mark centre with a light press.

Open up and then fold corner up to the centre mark on your first diagonal crease. Smooth crease firmly with your fingers.

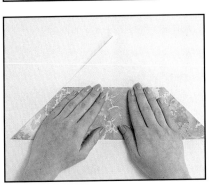

Fold again on original diagonal crease. Smooth down firmly with both hands.

Divide this fold into three and fold right-hand point over to meet first third, and left-hand point to meet new side fold. Smooth up side creases firmly. Fold back front point so that it meets left-hand fold and crease firmly.

Open up this triangle, so that it becomes a diamond, into which the top flap will tuck to close the envelope.

BIRTHDAY AND ANY OCCASION

We all love to receive birthday cards from friends and family — a sign that they remember and care for us. Children in particular are eager to remind us when their birthday is approaching. This gives us time to prepare a special card. The attraction of hand-made birthday or any occasion cards lies in their highly personal quality. Choose a motif to relate to a private joke or convey a special message. We offer here a wide variety of designs to suit different age groups, personalities and interests. Send a card at any time, just to say a special 'Hello', 'Thank you' or even 'Sorry I forgot'. Cards create a whole mood of their own, and our first is in full party swing.

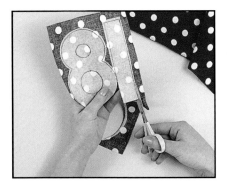

Trace out template 4 onto paper side of bonding web. Cut out just outside pencil outline. Iron onto wrong side of red polka dot fabric and cut out on pencil outline.

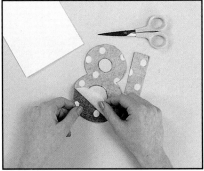

Peel off paper backing to reveal web of glue. Cut a piece of white card 14 by 24cm (5½ by 9½in). Score and fold 12cm (4¾in). Dry iron '18' onto front of card, making sure the '1' is on fold of card. The glue will melt with the heat of the iron. As long as card is not too light, ie, at least 240 gsm (160lb/sq in), the card will not curl.

Open out card and cut round edge of '18' leaving a tiny piece of card to hold together '1' and '8'. When drawing or cutting curves, it is always easier to work towards the body following curve of your hand.

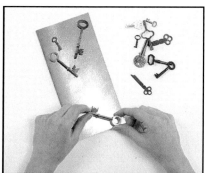

An unusual way to mark a 21st birthday and the traditional receipt of the key of the door. Cut a piece of bright silver card 22 by 22cm (8½ by 8½in) and score fold down the centre. Collect together some interesting shaped keys. Using a spray booth (see page 10), place folded silver card inside and lay keys on card in a pleasing arrangement.

Use spray car paint, holding the can 20-25cm (8-10in) away from card, and spray in a few short bursts to cover the whole card. Allow the first coat to dry for a few minutes and then spray a second coat. To ensure even distribution you should carefully turn the card between coats. You may wish to spray a third coat. Use in a well-ventilated room.

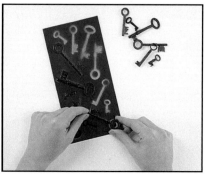

When completely dry, remove keys. You will not be able to get the cellulose paint off the keys easily, so be sure to use keys you no longer need. Other objects, such as old clock and watch parts, can also be used to make theme cards.

This card, in party mood, could be used for birthday, engagement or congratulations. Cut a piece of purple glossy card 20 by 30cm (8 by 12in). Score fold down centre of card (15cm/6in across). Cut two triangular shapes and bases from pink sequin waste and a piece of iridescent film to fit the width of the card. Mark with pencil dots where the glasses should be placed.

Using a spray booth, spray glue on to back of iridescent 'table' and smooth down to remove creases. Trim away any excess. Spray glue on to back of cocktail glasses and position on dot marks. Spray bases at the same time.

With a rubber-based glue, stick down strips of very narrow ribbon for stems, then bases. Curl two narrow pieces of ribbon, and place sequin 'bubbles' over glasses. A pair of tweezers will make this an easier task. Glue curls of ribbon on 'table' and leave for a few minutes for glue to set. Any residue may be gently rubbed away when dry.

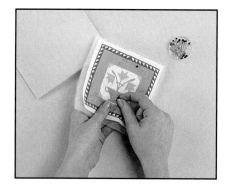

This small piece of quilting is from a ready-printed panel. It will shrink a little when it has been quilted, so measure and cut window from card *after* you have finished the piece. You will need very thin wadding (batting) to back the cotton panel. Cut a piece of card 45 by 15cm (18 by 6in) and score two folds 15cm (6in) apart. Pin panel to a slightly larger square of wadding.

On a larger piece of work, muslin would be used as a backing fabric, but in this instance it has been left out so that there is less bulk inside the card. Working from the centre, tack (baste) the two layers together, making sure the picture covers the wadding.

Cotton thread gives best results in hand quilting. Starting from the centre, with a knot on the back, sew with tiny running stitches. Finish thread with a double back stitch. Take out tacking stitches. Do not press or you will lose quilted effect. Measure finished piece and cut window from centre of 3-fold card. With double-sided tape, stick down quilted panel and back flap of card.

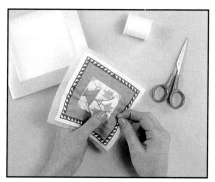

A window-box full of spring flowers is sure to bring cheer. We have used a ready-cut, 3-fold card with window. Fold under left-hand side of card (looking from the inside), marked with a cross in our second picture. With a sharp pencil, draw through window outline and cut out second window using a craft knife and steel ruler.

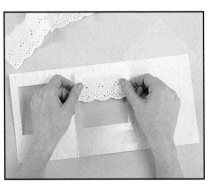

Place 1cm (½in) of double-sided sticky tape around centre window and edges of card. Cut piece of broderie anglaise or lace to fit half the window and a piece of tracing paper cut slightly larger than aperture. Peel off tape backing and stick down curtain, then tracing paper. Peel off tape backing on edges of card and close left-hand side over. Light will filter through.

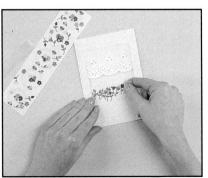

Apply 'stick-on' flowers (purchased on a strip) in a line half on the card and half on the tracing paper, then finish with a strip of satin ribbon or paper for the window box. Add a couple more flowers to the top of the window if you wish.

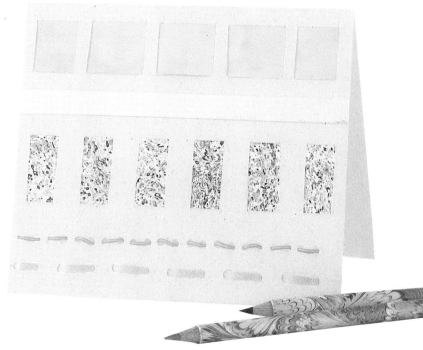

Cut card 15 by 25cm (6 by 10in). Score and fold 12.5cm (5in) across. On inside of card rule four sets of double lines and one single at each end, the depth of weaving strip. Use an even number of slits to start and finish on the inside. Vary depth for second line of slits. Rule two lines, one with 14 dots 9mm ($^3/_8$in) apart, second with 10 dots 16mm ($^5/_8$in) apart.

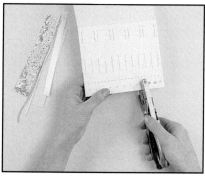

Any unusual papers can be used for weaving through the slits, particularly paper you have marbled yourself. Cut paper strips, ribbon and cord slightly longer than width of card, and carefully cut slits and punch holes.

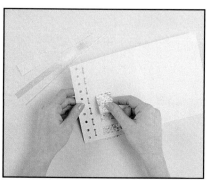

Still working from the inside weave paper, ribbon and cord and finish with a dab of glue. Trim any overhanging ends. On the front of card, glue a strip of ribbon between the two lines of woven paper.

B eautiful paper bags, too pretty to throw away, can be turned into greeting cards. Here, delicately-patterned wallpaper is used to advantage as a background. Cut card 20 by 30cm (8 by 12in). Score 15cm (6in) across and fold. With small scissors carefully cut out your favourite flowers and some leaves.

Cut wallpaper background, leaving small border of card showing. Mark a small dot at each corner with a sharp pencil, so you will easily be able to line up the background.

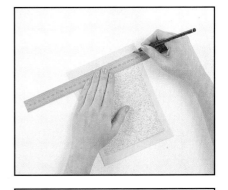

Spray glue on to background wallpaper and stick down on to card using pencil dots as a guide. Spray backs of roses and arrange. If you lay a clean sheet of paper over the card and smooth over the fresly-glued pieces, the edges will not catch on your hands.

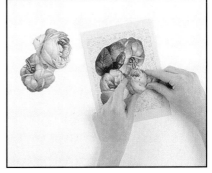

A lively teenage motif badge for sewing on to jeans and jackets makes a card and gift — it can be carefully peeled off the card at a later date and sewn on to a favourite garment. To put our pop singer in the spotlight we cut glossy red card 15 by 22cm (6 by 8½in). Score and fold 11cm (4¼in). Draw a spotlight shape on silver paper or plastic film using a ruler.

Cut out with a craft knife and trim the curve with a pair of small scissors.

First glue down the spotlight and trim any overhang on the edge of the card. Stick down the pop singer with rubber–based glue and hold firmly in place for a minute or two until glue dries. The discs on the main picture are buttons purchased from a specialist button shop (see page 120).

Cut blue card 23 by 16.5cm (9 by 6½in). Score and fold 11.5cm (4½in). Trace templates *5 and 6* for sail and windsurfer. Rub soft pencil over back of tracing of windsurfer, draw over outline again onto grey tissue-paper to transfer image and cut out. Make a template of the sail and draw round onto a piece of mid-blue card.

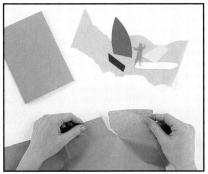

Draw and cut a surf-board from a piece of white card 10 by 1cm (4 by ½in) and curve ends. Cut out sail, and two coloured strips of card to fit diagonally over sail. Tear waves from two pieces of blue tissue-paper — one deep blue, the other a lighter blue. Glue coloured strips on to sail.

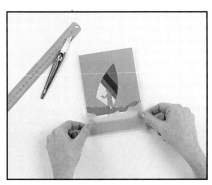

Arrange pieces on the main card and mark where they fit with sharp pencil dots. Place all components in spray booth right-side down and spray backs with glue. Place on card in order: dark waves then surf-board, sail, man and pale waves. Place a piece of clean paper over card and smooth pieces flat with your hand. Trim off any excess with craft knife.

D iagonal lines of spotted ribbon and self-adhesive labels give this card a 'dotty' air. Cut a piece of black card 25 by 16cm (10 by 6¼ in). Score and fold 12.5cm (5in). On inside top left-hand corner measure 4cm (1½ in) along top of card and down side edge, mark with dots and score. Fold corner back to outside of card.

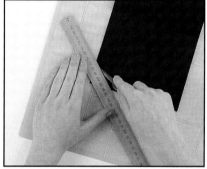

Rule a diagonal line across front of card from top left to bottom right. Measure and cut ribbons to fit either side of this line. Cut them slightly longer, to be trimmed later. Cut a triangle of ribbon to fit behind turned-down corner. Spray backs of ribbon with glue in spray booth. Place in position, smooth down and trim edges.

On front bottom left-hand corner of card, stick on self-adhesive dots and also on folded-over, top right-hand corner.

Colourful puffins, cut from a sheet of wrapping paper, keep a lookout from their perch. Cut card 28 by 13cm (18 by 5¼in). The card is blue on the inside and white on the outside. On the outside, from the left, score 9cm (3½in) and 19cm (7½in) across and fold. Turn card over and on the inside, from the left, score and fold 20cm (8in) across.

Cut out three puffins and spray glue the first on outside of far right-hand panel of card, facing right. Cut round him with a craft knife leaving him attached by his tail. The score line on the outside will allow him to stand forward.

Glue the other two puffins in place on the inside. Any wrapping paper with a distinct animal motif can be used in this way to make a striking card.

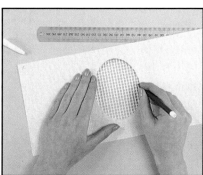

Offcuts of shot silk or other fabrics are woven into a landscape of green fields, hedges, yellow corn, blue sky and pink evening sunset. A ready-cut, 3-fold card was used. Mark top left-hand corner inside card with cross. Cut canvas about 10cm (4in) square. Lay card with oval aperture over canvas and mark edges lightly. Rule a square just outside these marks.

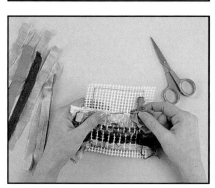

Cut stips of fabric approximately 1cm (½in) wide and 12.5cm (5in) long. Do not worry if they fray as this adds to the charm. Thread large tapestry needle and starting from the bottom weave green strips. Continue with yellow fields, hedges and sky.

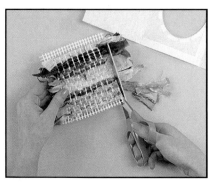

Attach double-sided tape around oval window and along three sides of panel, as shown. Trim canvas 6mm (¼in) outside the ruled square and peel off backing from double-sided tape. Stick canvas in place and close card — the left side with the cross is the side to fold in. Smooth from folded edge to outside so that card stays flat.

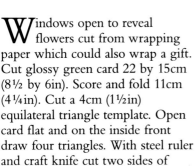

Windows open to reveal flowers cut from wrapping paper which could also wrap a gift. Cut glossy green card 22 by 15cm (8½ by 6in). Score and fold 11cm (4¼in). Cut a 4cm (1½in) equilateral triangle template. Open card flat and on the inside front draw four triangles. With steel ruler and craft knife cut two sides of triangles and score third.

Cut a piece of white paper the same size as the closed card and lay it under the card front. Open up windows and draw the triangles through the windows. These will be your guides for sticking on the pieces of flowered paper. Mark top left-hand corner of inside of card and paper with a cross. Cut out four triangles of flowers.

Glue flower triangles on paper where marked in pencil. Place a line of glue along all four edges on front of paper and attach face down on inside front of card. Open up the windows and you will see peeping flowers.

C ut out card 25 by 14cm (10 by 5½in). Score and fold 12.5cm (5in) across. Trace out fish (7, 8 and 9) on to the smooth side of bonding web. Cut out fish just outside pencil outline and place rough side of web on to back of your fabric. Press with a warm iron to melt the glue. Cut out on outline. Peel off backing and position on card. Press with a dry iron.

Draw in eyes and details of fish with felt-tipped pens. Alternatively, you can use sequins for the eyes. Cut rocks and stick down in place with spray glue.

Cut sea and sand from organza and put on to card with spray glue. Trim edges with a craft knife and use offcuts to make sea ripples and waves. **Note**: Be sure to use card of at least 240gsm (160lb/sq in) or the heat of the iron will distort it.

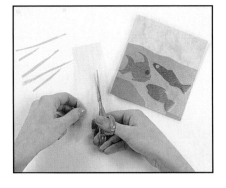

Cut nine heaps of lurex, silk and satin. Cut two pieces of acetate film 10cm (4in) and 9.5cm (3¾in). Draw a 7.5cm (3in) grid of 2.5cm (1in) squares with a chinagraph pencil. Use polyester thread and machine two centre horizontal lines and left-hand vertical. Stuff centre square. Machine right vertical to close centre square. Stuff squares on left; top and bottom centre.

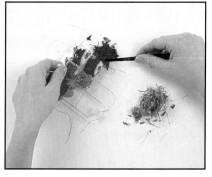

Machine left-hand edge, and then top and bottom edges to close squares. Stuff three right-hand squares and machine right-hand edge to close. Pull threads to back and knot. Trim and put a dot of glue on each knot to hold it.

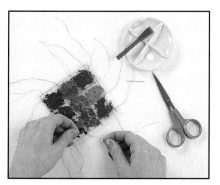

Make or buy a 3-fold card and cut a double window mount (see page 23). Mark inside top left-hand corner with cross. Put double-sided tape around centre window of card and edges. Pull off backing of tape and place patchwork parcels in window. Close card and add cord and tassel.

A theme card to give to a musical friend. The treble clefs are buttons. Cut red glossy card 22 by 15cm (8½ by 6in). Score and fold 11cm (4¼in). Draw a square 5.5 by 7.5cm (2¼ by 3in) on white paper. Rule two staves — groups of five lines 3mm (¹/₈in) apart — using a fine black felt-tipped pen. Cut out the square.

Centre the square of music paper on card so that you have an equal margin on three sides. Visually, it is better to have a larger margin at base of card. Mark corners of music lightly on card and stick down using spray glue. Place opened card on a piece of felt and pierce two holes for the two buttons using dividers or a thick needle.

From the back sew on buttons through the holes you have pierced, then knot the thread and trim. Finish knots with a dab of glue.

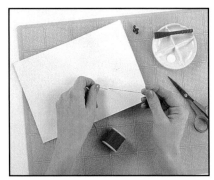

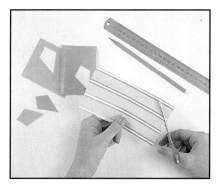

Kites flying in a high spring sky are always a cheerful sight and these three are made from wrapping paper and narrow satin ribbon. Cut pale blue card 22 by 15cm (8½ by 6in). Score and fold 11cm (4¼in). Cut out kites in three different sizes and papers using a ruler. Arrange and stick on card using spray glue.

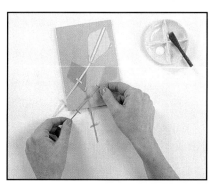

Cut narrow satin ribbons slightly longer than card so they will hang below bottom of card. Cut short lengths of ribbon for bows.

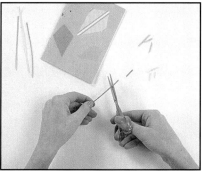

Glue and hold in place for a moment since satin ribbon tends to resist glue at first. Some of the bows can be a 'V' of twisted ribbon.

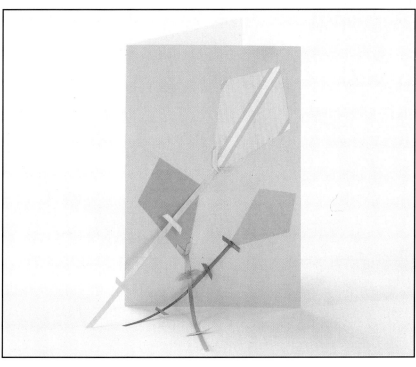

U se mono thread 'lockweave' needlepoint canvas 8 holes to 2cm or 10 holes to 1in, cut 18 by 14cm (7 by 5½in). Find centre of canvas and mark centre hole on four sides. Draw two crosses in different colours either side of centre and side holes. Without counting centre hole, count 29 holes either side lengthways and 18 widthways. Rule a border line.

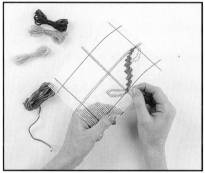

You will find a chart to follow on page 118. Thread a tapestry needle with either double-knitting wool or tapestry wool and counting holes, work long stitch in the pale lilac colour first.

Continue working towards centre, finishing four corners last. Cut a 3-fold card 45 by 20cm (18 by 8in), score and fold at 15cm (6in) intervals. Measure finished piece and cut a slightly smaller window in centre panel of card. Trim canvas to 6mm (¼in) all round and mount using double-sided tape. Close card and stick down.

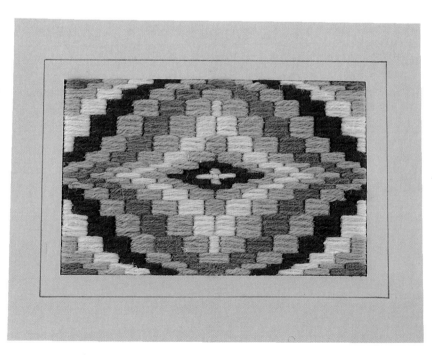

Cut card 22 by 22cm (8½ by 8½in), score and fold 11cm (4¼in) across. Centre your compass point horizontally 5.5cm (2in) from top of card. Draw an arc so that it touches the sides and top edge of card, then cut through both thicknesses. You could make a template of this shape if you wanted to make several cards.

Brightly coloured origami paper is perfect for this exuberant card. Either draw on back of paper or cut freehand a collection of shapes and colours.

Arrange paper shapes in order of gluing and stick them onto card. Tweezers will help you to apply glue to the tiny star shapes, not your fingers!

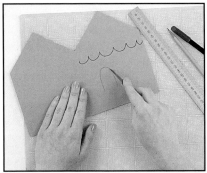

A detachable finger puppet of a jolly circus clown will delight a child. Cut card 18 by 25cm (7 by 10in). Score and fold 12.5cm (5in). Mark 5.5cm (2¼in) down sides of folded card. Measure across the top 6cm (2½in) and mark. Cut through both thicknesses of card to form apex of 'marquee'. Draw roof of marquee with felt-tipped pen. Cut a 'stand' for puppet on front of card.

Trace out templates *10, 11 and 12* and transfer onto thin card to make your own templates. Cut out two balloons from card and satin ribbon strings. Using turquoise felt, cut two hats, two hands and a bow-tie. Cut two heads from white felt; two circles, one for his nose and one for his hat, from pink felt. Cut eyes from narrow black satin ribbon.

Glue balloons and ribbons in place. Sandwich the clown's hands between the two pieces of felt for the head, holding in place with a dab of glue. Sew, with a running stitch, round the clown's head. Glue on hat, bobble, eyes, nose and bow-tie. Place clown on stand and he will appear to be holding the balloons.

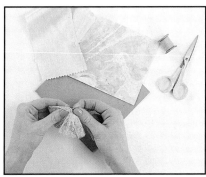

J ust the card to please a young girl who dreams of becoming a ballet dancer. Cut card 30 by 15cm (12 by 6in), score and fold 15cm (6in). Cut skirt from a piece of net 30 by 7.5cm (12 by 3in). Fold in half down its length and press with warm iron. Sew, with small running stitches, along this fold. Make a double stitch to start, gather tightly and finish with a double stitch.

Marbled paper is used for the background. Cut 13cm (5in) square. Cut mirror from silver paper or foil. Details of how to draw a curve are given on page 37. Cut bodice from satin and straps from satin ribbon.

Centre background paper and attach with spray glue. Then glue bodice and mirror. The straps will be easier to put on with rubber-based glue. Mark where skirt is to be attached and pierce two holes each side with dividers. Sew from back of card, tie knot and dab with glue. Make two more holes in the same way for the ballet shoes brooch. Finish with a silver star for a hopeful star.

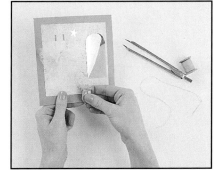

BOYS AND GIRLS COME OUT TO PLAY

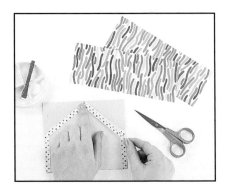

Cut card 30 by 13cm (12 by 5in), score and fold 15cm (6in). With fold on top find centre and mark with pencil dot. Measure down 6cm (2½in) on each side. Rule a line from each side point to middle mark to form roof. Stick down ribbon forming a mitre at apex of roof. Cut two pieces of medium weight wrapping paper 20 by 7.5cm (8 by 3in).

Trace out templates *14 and 15*. Fold length of wrapping paper in half then in half twice more. Draw on half boy or girl making sure hands are on folds. Cut out. When you draw the second child, check folds are in the opposite direction, so that when they are opened they are left and right of card. Open out boys and girls and refold alternate ways.

On green and pink paper cut a boy and girl. Glue them to the blank side of the folded figures. Glue the last girl and boy to the card so that their feet are on the bottom edge. Fold figures flat to fit in an envelope.

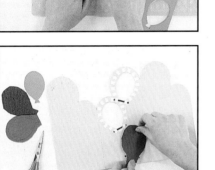

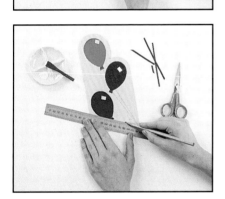

Cut yellow card 22 by 33cm (8½ by 12¾in). Score and fold 11cm (4¼in) and 22cm (8½in). Trace out template *13*, transfer to thin card to make template. Place over folded card, mark with sharp pencil around balloon outline at top and cut with sharp knife through all three thicknesses. Open out card and trace out balloon shapes onto centre panel and cut out.

Place double-sided tape in small pieces around the balloon holes on inside centre of card. Cut small pieces of narrow ribbon and stick across neck of balloons. Using balloon template, cut three satin balloons slightly larger. Remove double-sided backing and stick them in place. Stick down left side of the 3-fold card using double-sided tape.

Cut three 'reflection' squares out of white or silver fabric and glue on to the three balloons. Cut four lengths of narrow ribbon, one shorter, so that it will appear to pass behind the red balloon. Using a sharp pencil, rule guide lines for where the ribbons will be placed. Glue them down, leave for a minute or two for glue to dry and then trim ends.

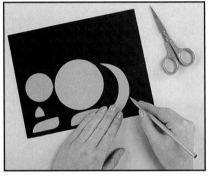

O ur mischievous black cat seems not to have noticed the little mouse! Cut card 23 by 18cm (9 by 7in), score 11.5cm (4½in) across and fold along top of card. Trace out cat templates *16-21* and transfer on to thin card to make your own templates. Draw around pieces on to black paper or card. Keep paws and tail the right way round.

Cut out black cat, a tree shape from tissue-paper or card and two green eyes. Mark with a sharp pencil where the pieces will fit on card and stick on in order using spray glue: the tree, body, paws, tail, ears and eyes.

Use stationers' self-adhesive dots for cat's nose and pupils. Finish by drawing whiskers using white chinagraph pencil. Draw around limbs and ears with a soft pencil to make cat stand out.

Cut card 30 by 20cm (12 by 8in), score and fold 15cm (6in) across. Trace out templates 22-25. Transfer designs onto thin card to make your own templates. Cut out from thin card two arms, two legs, head and body. From brown felt cut out same pieces but slightly larger. Glue felt to card — make a left and right leg. When glue is dry trim edges.

Tear green tissue-paper to resemble hills and hedges and cut gingham tablecloth. Glue them to card and position 'stick-on' flowers. Glue on Teddy's head and punch holes in body, arms and legs. Mark shoulder holes on card, since Teddy will be attached through them. Punch or cut out with a cross, so that brass paper-clips will pass through.

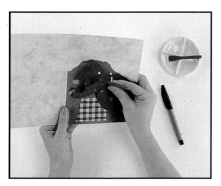

Join Teddy's legs to his body with brass paper-clips. Pass paper-clips through holes at top of Teddy's arms, body and card and open out on back to secure him. Glue on small black beads for eyes and nose. With a fine felt-tipped pen, draw in his snout and mouth.

CALENDAR EVENTS

The Christmas and New Year period is an important time for communication, re-affirming links with family and friends. And we all love to receive a stack of cards in the mail! Our pleasure is much increased when we receive a card made by hand, knowing the time, effort and thought involved in its production. Start sending hand-made cards for all calendar events and you will soon find that people will look forward to *your* cards in particular. We begin this section with card ideas for the 'festive season', followed by the key events throughout the year. Many of these designs could be adapted to suit more than one occasion.

Cut gold card 30 by 15cm (12 by 6in) and score twice 7.5cm (3in) in from each side. Trace out template *28* and carefully work out where the points will fall. Mark design on back of gold card and cut out using a sharp craft knife and ruler for straight edges.

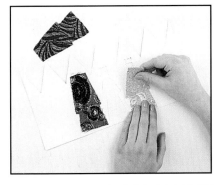

Burnish edges of gold card with the back of your thumbnail if they have lifted. Cut kings' clothes from three pieces of brocade, slightly larger than apertures. Place small pieces of double-sided tape around kings on inside of card and stick brocade in place.

Cut kings' gifts from gold card and glue in place. Attach sequins to points of their crowns. Stick on white card to cover back of centre panel. To protect the points, slip a further piece of card into the envelope. The three kings which have been cut out could be used for a further card, gift tag, or stencil.

C ut glossy red card 18 by 23cm (7 by 9in), score and fold 11.5cm (4½in) across. Cut on bias four strips of Christmas fabrics 2.5 by 30cm (1 by 12in) long. Fold strips lengthways, machine 3mm (⅛in) seam allowance. Leave length of thread at end, thread with bodkin and knot. Thread bodkin back through tube with damp fingers.

Thread length of double wool through each tube. Pin ends of tubes to a firm surface. Plait by laying four strands over left hand, take left strand over two middle strands and right strand over one. Continue to end. Ease into a circle, cross over ends and sew through to secure. Trim and finish with a bow.

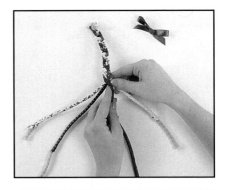

Bind trimmed ends with embroidery cotton, tie a knot and trim. Draw an arched border (see page 37) using a gold pen. Centre finished wreath and pierce through card with a thick needle or point of dividers. Sew through from back of card, knot thread, trim and finish with a dot of glue to hold firm.

O n red fabric draw in pencil
four 9cm (3½in) squares and
cut out. Fold in 6mm (¼in) seam
allowance and press. Find centre of
square by folding diagonally each
way and mark with tip of iron. Fold
down one corner to this mark and
pin. Continue with other corners to
make a square. Catch centre points
with a small stitch. Fold in again
and sew. Complete all four squares.

Cut four 2cm (¾in) squares from
fir-tree fabric. Place two red squares
right sides together and sew down
one side to make a double square.
Pin fir-tree patch diagonally over
seam on right side and curl back
folded edges surrounding patch. Slip
stitch to hold in place. Repeat to
make another double square.

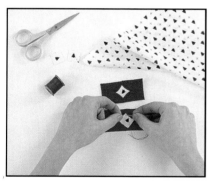

Sew double squares together and
place third and fourth fir-tree
patches over seams. Sew tiny beads
in corners of 'windows'. Cut card 25
by 18cm (10 by 7in), score and fold
12.5cm (5in). Mark top centre and
sides 6cm (2½in) down with pencil.
Cut through card to form a point.
Glue finished square centred
horizontally onto card. Add gold
border.

Cut card 18 by 23cm (7 by 9in). Score and fold 11.5cm (4½in). Draw border in silver pen around card. Trace off template *29* and transfer onto thin card. Draw round template onto red felt using a water-soluble pen. It is not easy to mark sequin waste so hold template in place and cut round it.

Sew sequin waste to felt by hand or machine, then trim both layers neatly.

Glue stocking to card, then add the little pony eraser or another small gift that can be glued on. Draw holly and berries using felt-tipped pens. You could also add beads and sequins if you wish.

CANDLELIT CHRISTMAS TREE

Cut card 15 by 20cm (6 by 8in) and score down centre. Trace template *32*, transfer onto thin card and draw round on green card. Cut out using craft knife. Set your sewing machine to a fairly wide satin stitch. Sew moving card from side to side to form garlands. Pull threads through to back, tie off with knot and finish with dab of glue.

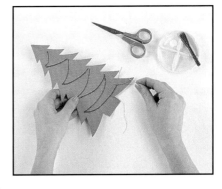

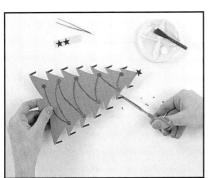

Stick on self-adhesive spots to resemble Christmas tree balls. Cut narrow satin ribbon into 14 1cm (½in) pieces.

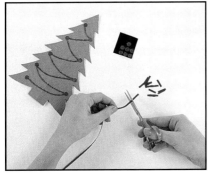

Glue them in place at end of branches on back of card. Tweezers will help you to hold them steady. Leave until glue dries. Cut tops diagonally to look like candles. Add the finishing touch — a red star on top of tree.

The snowman at the window invites us to come outside to play in the snow. Cut off left-hand side of this 3-fold card so that light will shine through window. Cut a piece of film slightly smaller than folded card. Draw snowman and trees on to paper to fit between window bars. Place paper under film and on right side draw outline of snowman and trees with silver pen.

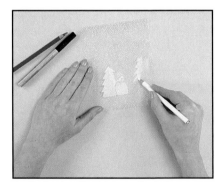

Turn over film and colour in trees and snowman using a white chinagraph pencil.

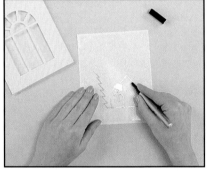

Turn back film onto right side and draw in scarf and nose with a red chinagraph pencil. Add face details in silver. Attach film to inside of card with double-sided tape and place a silver star where it can be seen shining through window.

A simple, easily-made card in unusual colours for Christmas. Cut card 11 by 20cm (4¼ by 8in), score and fold 10cm (4in). The fold is at the top of card. Cut a strip of green plastic from an old shopping bag. Tear four strips of tissue in shades of orange and yellow. The fir-tree is from a strip of self-adhesive 'stickers'.

Arrange strips so that colours overlap and produce new colours and tones. Stick down tree. Spray glue onto back of strips and stick down.

Trim excess paper from edges of card with a steel ruler and sharp craft knife.

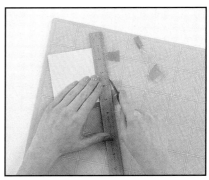

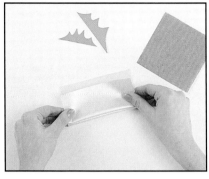

Cut silver card 30 by 15cm (12 by 6in), score and fold 15cm (6in). Trace templates *26 and 27* and transfer onto thin card. Cut 13cm (5in) square of green satin paper and 10cm (4in) square of dark green tissue-paper. Fold these two squares in half twice, then diagonally across to make a triangle.

Cut out larger holly from satin paper and unfold, then dark green holly. Hold holly templates in place on paper triangles with paper clips when cutting out. You can draw round the templates first if you find it easier.

Spray glue onto backs of holly leaves. Position the larger, pale green leaves first, then the dark green on top, between the pale green leaves. Stationers' self-adhesive spots make red berries. Put on five or so.

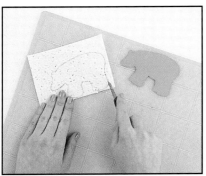

Cut card 23 by 18cm (9 by 7in), score 11.5cm (4½in) and fold along top. Trace out template *33* and transfer onto thin card to make template. Place on polystyrene wallpaper and draw round with a soft pencil. Cut out with craft knife. Cut out ice caps and ground from iridescent plastic or silver paper.

Glue down mountains, ground and polar bear, placing the latter in front of peaks. Glue on silver sequin stars.

With a silver pen, draw in polar bear's features: legs, paws and ears. The polar bear could also be made from white felt.

Cut card 15 by 22cm (6 by 8½in), score and fold 11cm (4¼in) along top. Mark centre top of the card with pencil dot. Cut triangle from sequin waste, place on card and mark two sides at bottom of tree. Glue along edges of tree and hold in place on card until glue dries. Any residue glue can be rubbed away when it is dry.

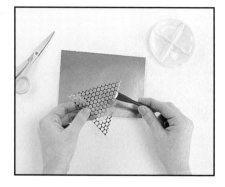

Cut a base for the tree from a piece of card or paper. Curl over scissors a number of narrow pieces of ribbon cut about 9.5cm (3¾in) long.

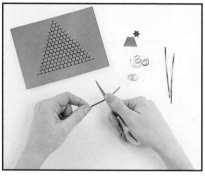

Glue on base and add sequin star to top of tree. Slip curled ribbons through every other hole in sequin waste and every other row, starting at top of tree. No need to tie them; they will stay in place. You will need to deliver this card by hand or use the boxes described on page 16.

The attraction of this card lies in combining circles cut from a variety of materials of a single colour. The feather adds a final touch of frivolity. Cut card 23 by 18cm (9 by 7in), score and fold 11.5cm (4½in). Find sequins of different sizes but similar colours, then paper, sequin waste, satin paper and foil. Sequin waste can be marked with dividers.

Draw circles of different sizes on your chosen materials. Any round objects can be used for this, or use a pair of compasses. Cut out.

Position circles and sequins to make an interesting arrangement and glue in place. Finally glue on a feather of matching colour.

A dove of peace for New Year. It is made from a paper doiley with calendar dates falling from its beak. Cut deep blue card 30 by 20cm (12 by 8in), score 15cm (6in) and fold. Draw freehand two curves at top of card to represent clouds and cut with craft knife.

Trace dove template *34* and transfer to thin card to make your own template. Trace out dove onto white paper doiley and cut out, together with dates 1 and 31 from an old calendar and strip of transluscent film waved along upper edge to resemble hills.

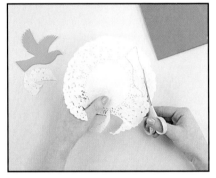

Spray glue all pieces and place on card together with four star sequins. Using a silver pen, draw line along edge of cloud curves.

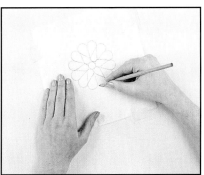

The card is a ready-made 3-fold with window. Cut out circle in left-hand section to match window (see page 23). Trace out template 35. Put masking tape in each corner to hold tracing still, then place silk over tracing, holding it firm with masking tape. Trace through onto silk using a soft pencil.

Place silk in an embroidery frame and draw over lines of design with gutta. This will stop the silk paints from running into each other. Leave to dry thoroughly — it may take an hour. A hairdryer will speed up the process.

Shake or stir fabric paints and using a clean damp brush flood each petal area with paint in one swift stroke. When paint is dry place a piece of fabric under silk and iron on wrong side for two minutes to set paint. Wash out gutta from silk and dry if you wish. Trim to just larger than window, stick down fabric and left-hand card section with double-sided tape.

New Year celebrations are particularly associated with Scotland. So here, in traditional Scottish style, we have tartan and golden bells for our New Year greeting. A ready-cut window card was used. Remove left-hand section of 3-fold card with a sharp craft knife and ruler. Use this spare card to make two bells.

Cut a piece of tartan fabric or paper to fit inside back of card, attach with spray glue and trim edges. Trace template 30 and transfer on to spare gold card. Cut out and back with tartan using spray glue. Trim with small scissors. Punch holes in bells.

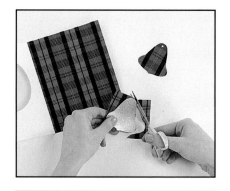

Make a bow from narrow satin ribbon and cut a length for the bells to hang from. Thread first bell and hold in place with a dab of glue. Thread second bell. Sew through bow and ends of the bell's ribbon to hold in place, glue at top of circular window, so that bells hang free.

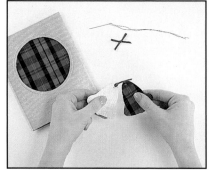

This card could be used for the New Year or Christmas. You will see from template *31* that only two sides of the 3-sided card are shown. The left-hand portion is a repeat of the right but with 7cm (2¾in) added to the bottom, so it stands taller. Trace out template adding extra section to make left-hand part of card. Rub soft pencil over back of tracing.

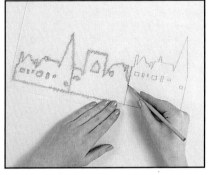

Cut a piece of white card 33 by 15cm (13 by 6in), lay tracing over right side up, lining up lower edges, hold in place with masking tape and draw over outline to transfer drawing.

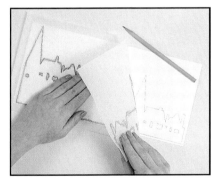

Use a ruler to help keep lines straight and cut out. Score and fold into sections. Trim lower edge and 1mm (¹/₁₆ in) from one side of card so that it will fold flat. You will need an extra piece of card in the envelope to protect the points.

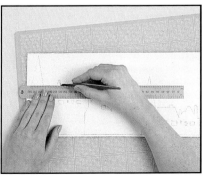

Cut card 22 by 15cm (8½ by 6in), score and fold 11cm (4¼in). Trace out heart *37* and transfer to a thin piece of card to make your own template. Cut out a heart in thin white card. Place template on front of card at a slight angle and draw round in pencil. Cut round pencil line leaving enough uncut at bottom to enable card to stand.

Glue dried flower petals on to white heart working in rows from outside to centre. Use a rubber-based glue; tweezers will help to hold petals steady. Finish with a whole flower in centre.

Cut border from a paper doiley. Spread a thin line of glue on outside of main card heart. Pleat doiley border onto glue all round heart. Stick petal heart over pleated doiley, cover with a piece of clean paper and smooth down. Hold for a minute until glue dries. Lastly stick on Victorian angel motif on top right-hand corner of card.

We used a mould from a cake decorating shop and filled it with tiny cake sweets. Cut a 3-fold card 42 by 19cm (16½ by 7½in), score and fold 14cm (5½in). Tape heart to back of tracing paper. Turn over and rub along edge of heart with soft pencil to make template. Line up heart tracing in centre of middle section of card and transfer outline. Cut out with craft knife.

Place double-sided tape round heart aperture and around edges of left-hand portion of card, marked with a cross. Remove backing from tape around heart and place mould in position. Press to stick firmly. Put narrow line of double sided-tape around edge of heart.

Pour sweets into heart until full and pack out with a piece of wadding (batting) cut to heart shape. Take off backing from tape around heart and from left-hand portion of card, fold over card and press down. A pretty pink bow is the finishing touch.

A doll's straw bonnet forms the basis of this card and is decorated with spring-coloured ribbons, flowers and a butterfly. Cut card 15 by 22cm (6 by 8½in), score and fold 11cm (4¼in). Cut length of yellow ribbon and cut inverted 'V' shape at ends. Hold in place around hat and sew leaving tails at centre back. Repeat with a length of slightly narrower ribbon.

Trim stems of small fabric flowers and pin in place on ribbon at regular intervals around hat.

Sew flowers in place using double thread. Finish with butterfly at front. Centre bonnet on card and attach by sewing through brim of hat and knotting threads on inside of card. A dab of glue will make knots secure. Arrange ribbons prettily.

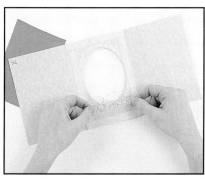

U se a ready-made 3-fold card with oval, egg-shaped window. Place double-sided tape around oval window and edges of inside of card. Peel off backing and attach strip of gold lace to bottom of oval. Cut piece of sumptuous satin slightly larger than aperture, and stick down so that the satin side will show through window.

Glue large, jewel-like bead in centre of 'egg'. Arrange beads, sequin leaves and petals, then glue in position. Tweezers will make it easier to place them accurately.

Finish with smear of rubber-based glue around edge of egg on outside of card. Leave for a moment to become tacky, then press down gold braid. Neatly trim end of braid.

A fun 'spook' for Halloween, quickly and easily made from paper and sequins. Cut red card 22 by 16cm (8½ by 6¼in). Score and fold 11cm (4¼in). Trace out templates *39* and *40* and make your own templates. Cut out witch's hat from black paper or card. Cut pumpkin head from orange paper or card, then cut out eyes and mouth.

Position head and hat on card and mark with a sharp pencil. Glue pieces in place.

Add sequin stars and moons using rubber-based glue, holding them in place for a moment while glue dries. Tweezers make handling the sequins easier.

The flowers we used are Victorian scrap or motifs. You could also cut flowers from magazines or old birthday cards. Cut card 25 by 19cm (10 by 7½in), score and fold 12.5cm (5in) for top of card. Trace out template *42*. Place tracing over gold card and draw again using a sharp pencil which will indent soft gold card.

Measure a border around edges of card and mark in pencil. Go over border again in gold pen.

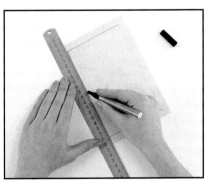

Glue the cornucopia onto the card, then the flowers and fruit tumbling out. Add a white dove.

A lace sachet of pot pourri could be detached and used later to perfume a drawer. Pot pourri can be bought in a variety of colours and perfumes. Cut card 23 by 18cm (9 by 7in), score and fold 11.5cm (4½in). Cut out two lace flowers, pin together and oversew leaving a gap to fill with pot pourri.

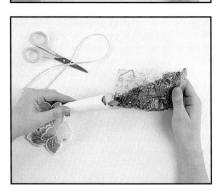

Make a funnel from a piece of paper and fill lace sachet with pot pourri. Oversew to close. Make a bow from narrow satin ribbon and curl ends over scissors.

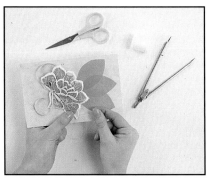

Cut three tissue paper leaves and glue onto card. Sew bow on to sachet. Using a point of dividers or a thick sharp needle, make two holes at either side of card, for positioning sachet. Sew through and knot on back, securing with a dab of glue.

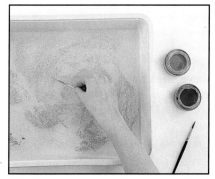

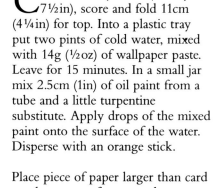

Cut card 22 by 19cm (8½ by 7½in), score and fold 11cm (4¼in) for top. Into a plastic tray put two pints of cold water, mixed with 14g (½oz) of wallpaper paste. Leave for 15 minutes. In a small jar mix 2.5cm (1in) of oil paint from a tube and a little turpentine substitute. Apply drops of the mixed paint onto the surface of the water. Disperse with an orange stick.

Place piece of paper larger than card gently on top of water and remove again fairly quickly, as soon as the paint has taken to surface of paper. Leave to dry on a sheet of newspaper. Press flat, if necessary, when dry. Cut to fit card and glue down.

Trace out car from a magazine or postcard and transfer to glossy white paper. Cut out and glue down. Trace 'chrome' details on to silver paper or card, cut out and glue in place. Add details with silver pen.

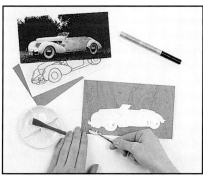

SPECIAL OCCASIONS

By 'special occasions' we mean those important milestone life events which deserve to be marked in suitable style. We start with the most momentous of all — being born! — to passing examinations and a first or new job. Then there are the big romantic events — engagement, the wedding day and anniversaries. We have also included cards to celebrate a new home, retirement and going on holiday. The card designs can be additionally personalized by adding decorative initials, for example to the engagement doves. It is easy to frame cards using clip frames without a border but a mount cut to size. You can also use frames which simply lock in place.

This card is worked in cross-stitch over hardanger fabric, 22 holes to 2.5cm (1in). Use six colours of stranded cotton, two strands thick. Mark centre of fabric by folding in half and running a tacking stitch along fold in both directions through holes. You will find a chart to work from on page 119.

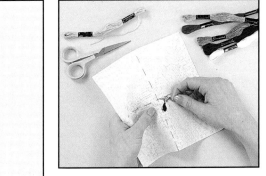

It is best to work one quadrant at a time, starting at the centre where guidelines cross. Work bottom diagonals of cross-stitch first, then return in opposite direction to form cross. This helps to get an even stitch since the thread tends to wear thin. Do not start with a knot but sew over ends on back as you work. Finish in same way.

When complete, remove guideline stitches. Press back of work using a pressing cloth and trim. Cut card to frame oval template *36*, score and fold in half. Cut oval window in front. Mount work with double-sided tape and back with a piece of white paper to fit. Attach with double-sided tape.

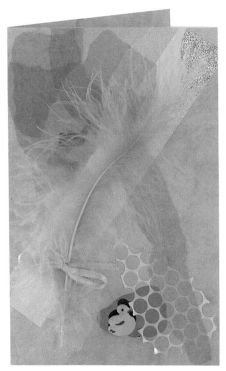

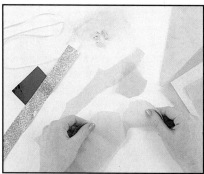

Cut card 23 by 18cm (9 by 7in), score and fold 11.5cm (4½in). This is a spontaneous arrangement, so no two cards will look the same. Lay out a selection of blue materials: ribbon, sequin waste, buttons, feathers, tissue and silver paper. Tear tissue-paper and cut chosen papers into random shapes. When you overlay strips of tissue, more shades of blue will occur.

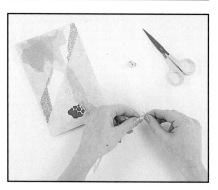

Spray glue your materials and place in your favourite arrangement and trim any excess. Tie a bow from narrow satin ribbon onto base of feather and trim ends diagonally. Attach to card by sewing through.

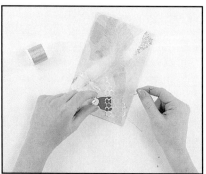

To attach duck button, make two holes with sharp needle or point of dividers, checking which way the button shank lies. Sew on duck button from back using double thread. Finish with a knot and secure with a dab of glue.

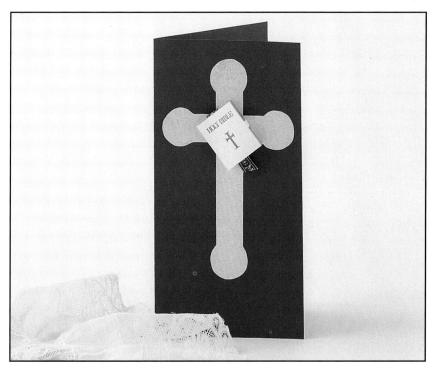

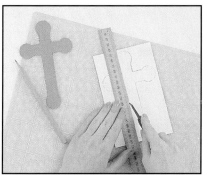

The tiny Bible is from a doll accessories' supplier. Cut card 23 by 22cm (9 by 8½in), score and fold 11cm (4¼in). Trace cross template *41* and transfer onto thin card to make your own template. Trace out onto gold paper and cut straight edges with a craft knife and ruler. The curved ends can be cut with scissors.

Lay template on card to position cross and mark with pencil. Spray glue on wrong side of cross and attach to card.

Stick a piece of double-sided tape on back of Bible, peel off backing and attach to cross at an angle.

GRADUATION TROPHY

Cut grey marble–effect card 28 by 19cm (11 by 7½in), score and fold 14cm (5½in). Trace out template 43. Cut piece of silver card to fit, turn over and hold down with masking tape. Place tracing over card and attach with masking tape. Trace through onto card with a sharp pencil. Trace base onto a piece of black card.

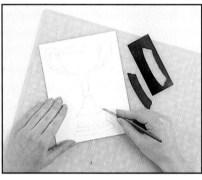

With a sharp craft knife, cut out cup and base. Burnish edges of silver card by rubbing gently with the back of your thumbnail.

Glue cup onto card with spray glue and draw in details with a sharp hard pencil. Finally, glue on base.

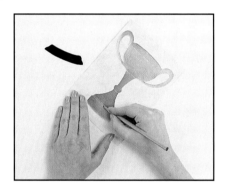

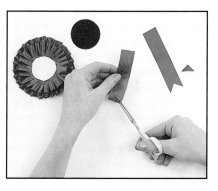

C ut a circle of card 3cm (1¼in) in radius. Take approximately 1 metre (3ft 2in) of single-sided 2.5cm (1in) wide pink satin ribbon, pleat and machine sew round edge of card circle. Machine an inner circle of pleated blue ribbon. A wide zig-zag stitch will hold pleats in place. Fold ends under to finish. Keep excess lengths of ribbon.

Cut a circle of pink metallic paper or card 2.2cm (⁷/₈in) in radius. Using left-over ribbon, cut two tails, one from each colour and one longer than the other. Cut an inverted 'V' shape at ends.

Cut metallic card 23 by 18cm (9 by 7in), score and fold 11.5cm (4½in). Glue tails in place over ends of pleated ribbon. Glue circle of pink paper or card in centre of rosette. Attach rosette to card with glue.

Cut green card 22 by 15cm (8½ by 6in), score and fold 11cm (4¼in). Cut piece of traditional ledger-look marbled paper 15 by 9cm (6 by 3½in). Cut away top and bottom right-hand corners by measuring 4cm (1½in) along top and right-hand edges and bottom and right-hand edges.

Spray glue on back of paper and attach to card so that there is a 2cm (¾in) margin of green card on left-hand side. Punch a hole in centre along right-hand edge of front of card.

Thread a length of brown satin ribbon through hole and tie into a bow.

Purchase a 3-fold window card in a pale colour whichever size you prefer. Mark inner left-hand portion of card with a cross. Select an attractive picture, or focus on a detail, from a magazine and lay window over picture. Mark four edges and corners with pencil dots.

Cut out picture slightly larger than window. Place double-sided tape around edges of window inside card and stick down picture using pencil guide marks to position. Fold over and stick down left-hand portion of card using double-sided tape.

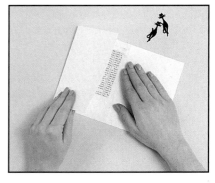

The cats are purchased from a bead shop and attached to card with rubber-based glue. Hold in place for a minute or two until glue dries.

Make your own template from our dove *(46)* and cut an extra template for wing alone (see finished card). Draw round dove twice on dark blue felt so that birds face opposite directions and cut out. Cut two pieces of muslin 18 by 11.5cm (7 by 4½in), position doves between two layers and pin. Tack layers together to hold doves in place.

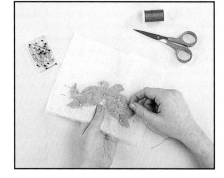

Using two strands of embroidery thread, sew tiny running stitches around doves and stitch feet (see finished card). Place wing template over doves and lightly draw round with a sharp pencil. Quilt along these lines. When finished, take out tacking thread and lightly press.

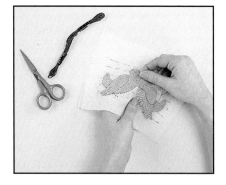

Purchase a 3-fold window card to fit quilted doves. Cut out matching window from left-hand section of card (see page 23). Trim muslin to about 6mm (¼in) larger than window. Check and mark top of window to avoid mounting work upside-down. Stick down using double-sided tape. Add tiny round beads for doves' eyes and pearl beads to corners of window.

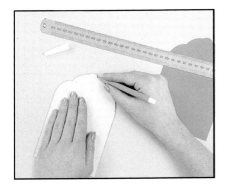

Cut card 22 by 16cm (8½ by 6¼in), score and fold 11cm (4¼in). Trace out template *48* and transfer to thin card adding 10cm (4in) to depth, to match card. Cut out and place on folded card. Draw round church window shape at top of card and cut through both thicknesses. Draw border with felt-tipped pen using ruler for straight edges.

Place several layers of different shades of pink tissue-paper together in a pile on a cutting board. Cut round template *38* to make approximately 10 hearts.

Spray glue hearts and position on card so that they overlap. You could stick more hearts inside card and also leave some loose so that they scatter when card is opened.

Colours can be matched to those of the bridesmaid's dresses. Cut card 15 by 30cm (6 by 12in), score and fold 15cm (6in). Bind turquoise felt-tipped pen to compass and draw a double circle on centre of card. Sew a line of running stitches along edge of strip of lace half a metre (1ft 6in) in length. Gather into a circle and sew seam.

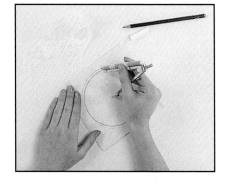

Sew ribbon flowers onto centre of lace circle. Cut a strip of flower braid into single flowers and sew around ribbon flowers.

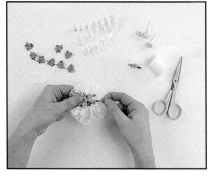

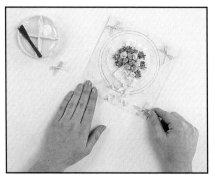

Sew on a couple of strings of ribbon flowers or braid to hang from bouquet. Using a sharp needle or compass point, make several holes in card and sew on lace bouquet from back of card using double thread. Tie a knot and add a dab of glue to secure. Glue on satin bows in four corners.

Cut card 30 by 15cm (12 by 6in), score and fold 15cm (6in). Trace template 47 and transfer to piece of white card. Cut piece of white card 2.5 by 9cm (1 by 3½in) and score across 1.25cm (½in), 2.5cm (1in), 4cm (1½in) and 1.25cm (½in) for stand. Decorate cake using felt-tipped and silver pens before cutting out.

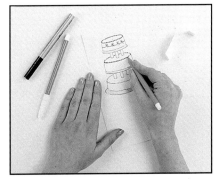

Glue down doiley tablecloth on base of card. In pencil, draw two lines 2.5cm (1in) either side of fold in centre. This is your guide for placing cake stand. Glue 4cm (1½in) section to back of cake, then place bottom 1.25cm (½in) section on guide line and glue. Glue silver bows, bells and horseshoes in place.

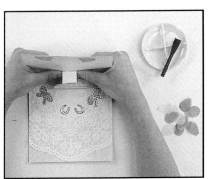

Glue final 1.25cm (½in) section of stand to back of card and hold until glue dries. Cut some tissue-paper confetti in colours to match cake, glue some to tablecloth and leave some loose. Punch holes in four corners of card. Thread curled silver ribbon through to tie and close card.

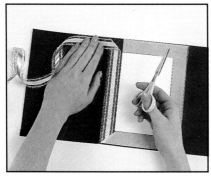

Cut a piece of blue foil card 45 by 20cm (18 by 8in). Score at 15cm (6in) and 30cm (12in) across and fold on outside. Cut out centre window 10 by 15cm (4 by 6in). On outside place double-sided tape around window. Stick down silver ribbon. Mitre corners by folding back ribbon at right-angles and cutting diagonally. Cut next piece of ribbon at same diagonal to fit.

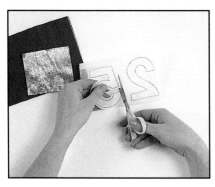

Trace template 53 onto paper side of bonding web, then cut out. Iron rough side onto silver lamé and when cool cut out carefully. Peel off tracing paper, turn over and iron onto a piece of silk or satin 11 by 16.5cm (4½ by 6½in), placing numbers so that they overlap.

Set machine to satin stitch and test on spare piece of fabric. Use silver thread on top and polyester thread on bobbin. Use an appliqué or buttonhole foot if you have one. If fabric puckers, place a piece of paper under fabric. When finished knot threads at back. Mount, using double-sided tape and close card.

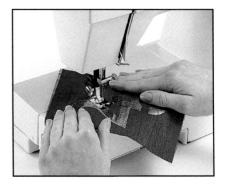

A bunch of golden roses to celebrate 50 golden years together. Cut card 16.5 by 25cm (6½ by 10in), score and fold 12.5cm (5in). Find horizontal centre of card and draw a circle with gold pen taped to compass. Cut three 10cm (4in) pieces of gold gift-wrap ribbon and cut ends diagonally to use as leaves.

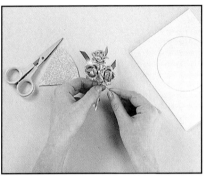

Arrange gold roses with leaves and hold in place by binding together with fine wire. Cut a piece of gold paper in a triangle shape, curving the top.

Wrap paper around flowers and glue at back to secure. You may like to put a dab of glue to hold roses in place. Apply glue to back of bunch of flowers and stick in place on card. Add golden birds and hearts and a large '50' cake decoration.

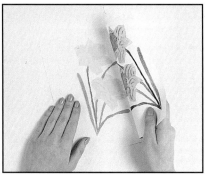

Cut card 22cm (8½in) square, score and fold 11cm (4¼in). Cut out a window 9 by 16.5cm (3½ by 6½in). Trace daffodils from a catalogue or book and transfer onto cartridge paper. Paint with transfer paints. When dry, place over square of polyester or poly-cotton fabric and press with a hot dry iron for two minutes. Carefully lift off paper.

Place print in an embroidery frame the opposite way from hand embroidery and pull until taut. To machine embroider, use same thread on top and bobbin. Take off presser foot and drop 'feed dog' so that teeth will not hold work and you will be able to move it freely. Place embroidery ring under needle and drop pressure leaver.

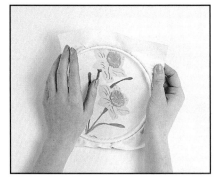

Moving machine wheel by hand, draw up bobbin thread to top and hold to start. Move ring, keeping your fingers on edge of frame and slowly paint with your needle. Experiment with stitches — length 0 and zig-zag are good. Sew outline first then colour in. Press on reverse, mount with double-sided tape and back with white paper.

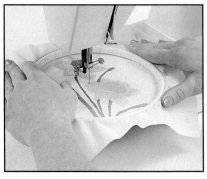

Cut card 22 by 15cm (8½ by 6in), score and fold 11cm (4¼in). Trace templates *44 and 45* and transfer onto green card for bedhead, and brown for bunny's head. Cut them out and an oblong of white paper for a pillow. Trim edges of pillow with pinking shears.

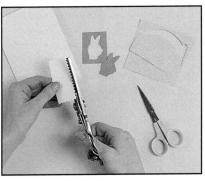

On good quality cartridge paper, draw a patchwork quilt and fill in squares with transfer paint following manufacturer's instructions. Iron painting onto a piece of bonded interfacing or man-made fabric and trim to fit bed.

Spray glue backs of all pieces and attach to card in order: bedhead, pillow, bunny and quilt. Draw in bunny's features with a fine felt-tipped pen. Add wallpaper pattern using groups of four dots to look like flowers.

Cut card 45 by 20cm (18 by 8in). Score and fold at 15cm (6in) and 30cm (12in) to form 3-fold. Follow chart on page 118. You may vary the wools and use up odds and ends. Most wool is used double on 12 holes to 2.5cm (1in) canvas. Find centre point of canvas and draw on fireplace design with felt-tipped pens.

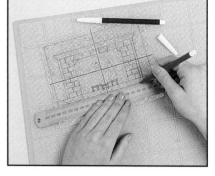

Start in centre, working the fire in random long stitch and tent stitch, varying the colours of the flames. Next, work the fire basket in tent stitch.

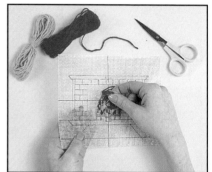

Continue with copper fireguard in slanting satin stitch, fire surround in tent stitch, brickwork in long stitch, carpet in tent stitch and walls in long stitch. For the rug, lay a cocktail stick across canvas and work stitches over stick. Cut loops to make pile. When finished, trim and cut a window in 3-fold card to fit piece. Mount with double-sided tape.

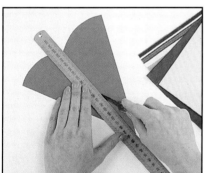

I dyllic leisure-filled days, beachcombing in yellow sand under blue sky. Trace template 51 and transfer to blue card. Score down centre.

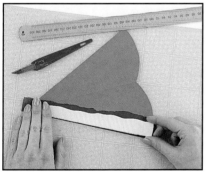

Tear blue tissue-paper to resemble sea. Cut a piece of yellow paper with a curved top edge to make it appear that waves are breaking. Place pieces wrong side up in a spray booth and spray glue. Fix to card and trim to fit.

Cut a piece of striped fabric or paper to make a beachtowel. Draw fringe on towel with a felt-tipped pen. Glue in place. Punch two holes and insert beach umbrella.

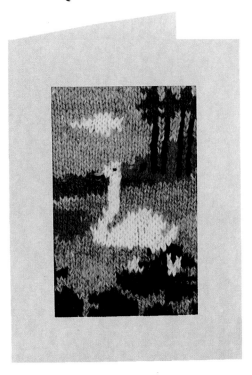

Cast on 36 stitches and knit in stocking stitch using 4-ply wools, following chart on page 119. Weave different-coloured yarns at back by laying new yarn just under right-hand needle and looping wool for next stitch around it without making an extra stitch.

When piece is finished, block it out before pressing on wrong side into a soft surface. Pin all round edges without stretching piece. Press using a damp cloth or steam iron. Leave to settle.

Sew in beak, using yellow wool, and his eye using black wool. Cut card 45 by 20cm (18 by 8in). Score and fold at 15cm (6in) and 30cm (12in) to form 3-fold card. Measure and then cut a window in centre portion. Use double-side tape to attach knitting and close card. Make sure you mount swan the right way up.

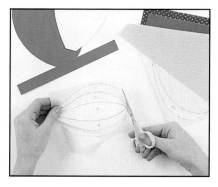

Trace out template *52* and transfer outer balloon onto blue card, inner balloon onto white card and also onto tracing paper side of bonding web. Number each segment and cut out. Mark on blue balloon where inner balloon will fit. Iron balloon segments onto wrong side of three fabrics. Cut out carefully and peel off backing.

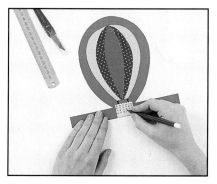

Place balloon segments onto white card balloon and press with a dry iron. Trim edges and using guide on main blue balloon, glue down. Cut a small piece of fabric for basket with pinking shears and glue in place.

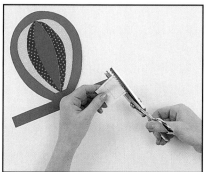

Draw in ropes then basket design on fabric using a brown felt-tipped pen. Score base of balloon where indicated on right side and fold back so that the balloon will stand. If being mailed, this card should have an extra piece of card in the envelope for protection.

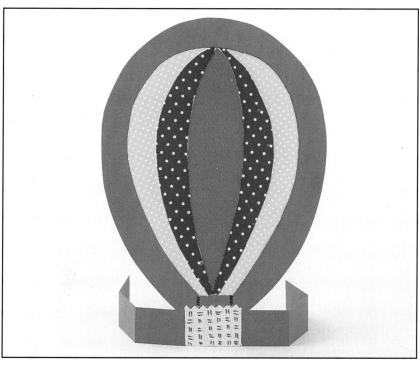

On good quality cartridge paper, draw a 12cm (4¾in) square. Using a postcard or photograph as a guide, roughly draw in mountains, lakes, trees and grass. Colour in with transfer paint, applied sparingly. The colours will not be true to the end product since they will change according to fibre content of material on which you print.

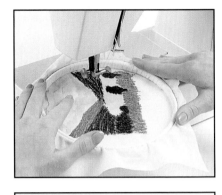

When paint is dry, place paper over poly-cotton and press for two minutes with a hot dry iron. Try not to move paper. You can make several prints from one painting. Mount the picture in an embroidery ring as shown. Follow your sewing machine's instructions for free machine embroidery. Using a selection of threads, fill in areas using satin stitch and straight stitch.

Tie ends of satin stitch on back when finished and press. Cut card 14 by 28cm (5½ by 11in). Cut a window 11.5cm (4½) square. Attach finished picture behind window using double-sided tape, then cut a piece of white backing paper and attach to back of your work. Trim excess paper.

Cut card 22 by 15cm (8½ by 6in), score and fold 11cm (4¼in). Draw border around card, first in pencil then pink felt-tipped pen. Roll out a piece of white Fimo modelling material until thin and cut a kite shape. Cut edges again with pinking shears.

Roll out lots of tiny pink balls for flowers and some long green sausages to be cut for stems. Roll out some flat lengths of pink clay to make bow.

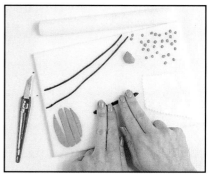

Fashion wrapping paper shape from 'kite' and place on piece of baking foil. Slip green stems inside and press on flower balls with cocktail stick. Make bow by folding pink lengths and shaping. Lay on foil and bake for 15-20 minutes on 130°C (275°F/Gas mark 1) to harden (check manufacturer's instructions). Leave to cool, glue to card and attach bow.

—QUICK AND SERIES CARDS—

We thought you would appreciate a section on quickly-made cards for occasions such as Christmas, where you need to produce multiples. But with these hand-crafted designs, everyone will receive a 'unique' card in the series. Make several of these cards to keep in stock for busy times or unexpected events. How often have you wanted to send a really special card and not had the time available? Single cards can be made quickly and easily using select materials and a strong basic design. Some of these cards could be used as invitations to a dinner party or some other social event, adapted to reflect the colour scheme or theme of the occasion.

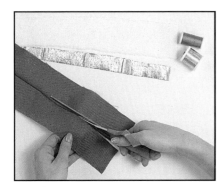

To make these quick cards even speedier to achieve, we used ready-cut 3-folds, and stickers and buttons to decorate. Cut three strips of fabric in suitable colours: here, blue glitter-spotted material for sky, silver lamé for frozen landscape and white towelling for snow.

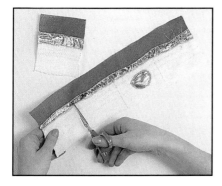

Machine the strips together with a wide satin stitch. Machine over twice if you want a thicker line. Measure size of aperture of ready-cut 3-fold cards and mark cutting lines on fabric. Machine trees with lines of stitch, or cut circles of lamé and make ponds. Let your imagination dream up a different idea for each card.

Cut up sections and sew buttons in place or attach stickers. Using double-sided tape, mount pieces and close cards. Extra sequins can be added to borders for moon or stars.

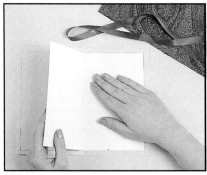

Beautiful wrapping paper lasts a little longer made into a quick and effective card. Cut card, score and fold. Cut wrapping paper a little larger. Glue wrong side of wrapping paper and lay it flat. Position first half of card on paper and smooth. Bring up wrapping paper to adhere to other half of card but leave room for fold. Smooth down.

Trim edges with a sharp knife. Affix ribbon on four sides on inside of card with a little piece of double-sided tape. Tie ribbon in a bow.

Photographs of flowers can be mounted on cards and sent to friends during winter months. Make a collection over the summer. Make a mask of the right size so that you may frame the most effective image. Mark four corners with a compass or sharp pencil point. Cut off excess with ruler and craft knife. Spray glue to mount.

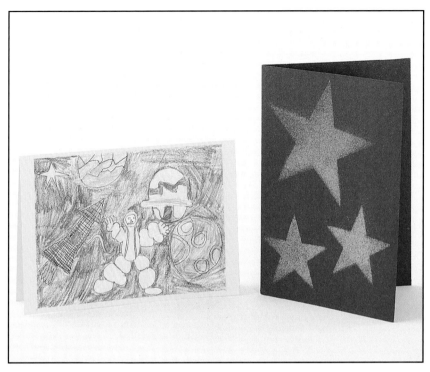

Stencilling is a good way of making several cards quickly. We used gold spray paint — remember to use a spray booth. Stencil card is firm and flat so the paint does not spread under the edges. Cut a piece of stencil card large enough to cover cards. Using templates *49 and 50*, cut out stars with a sharp knife and ruler.

Shake can of paint for a minute or two, then spray from a distance of 30cm (12in). A couple of coats gives a deeper colour and paint dries quickly. The stars you have cut from the stencil can also be used to make reverse image cards.

Our cosmonaut was drawn by a six year-old boy. Draw several squares 9 by 14cm (3½ by 5½in) and ask a child to draw some pictures. Choose her or his favourite and photocopy it several times. The child will have great fun colouring in these drawings, perhaps each one in different colours. Cut card mounts to fit and stick down drawings.

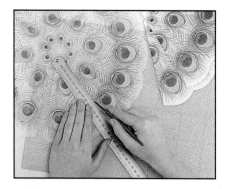

G ossamer-fine Japanese paper napkins make quick cards. Simply cut out designs and glue them to cards. With a sharp craft knife, cut a fan shape from a circular peacock napkin, so that the two large 'eyes' are at top. Spray glue back of fan, position and smooth onto card.

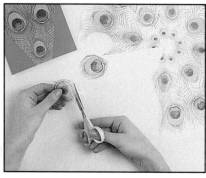

Cut two further eyes from napkin. Arrange, spray glue wrong side and smooth down onto card.

Experiment with different designs and cards to highlight the subtle colours. Butterflies on gold make an exotic card.

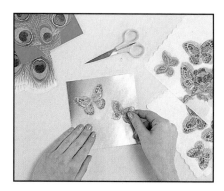

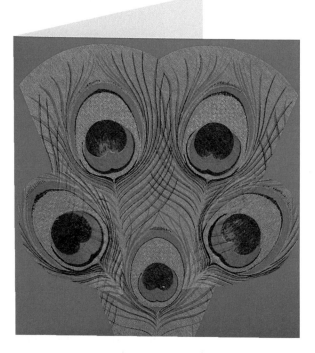

This magical, ever-rolling landscape is all in the imagination. It is made from layers of torn tissue-paper and plastic iridescent film. Cut pieces of card 16 by 25cm (6¼ by 10in). Score and fold 12.5cm (5in). Roughly tear several strips of tissue-paper and cut iridescent film.

Arrange them on a sheet of A4 (21 by 30cm/8 by 12in) typing paper so that colours overlap and shade. When you are happy with your arrangement, turn strips over and spray glue. You will find one side of tissue-paper has more shine than the other. If there are gaps, you could fill them in with silver pen.

Divide sheet of paper into six or more pieces and cut with a sharp craft knife. Each landscape can now be positioned on a card and glued.

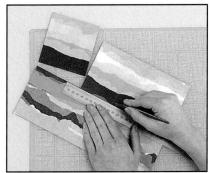

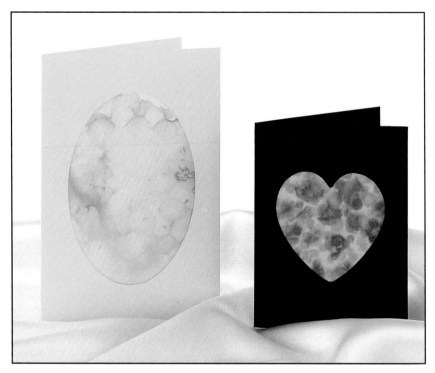

Wonderful abstract patterns can be produced by sprinkling salt on freshly painted silk. Cut a piece of fine white silk lining and place in an embroidery frame, pulling taut. Select colours of silk paints you wish to use, shake and carefully open jars. Wet brush in water jar. Apply paint fairly swiftly and immediately sprinkle on salt. Fill frame with designs.

Leave to dry, then brush off salt. The silk will yield a variety of effects, so place different ready-cut window cards over the most attractive patterns. Mark area to be framed in window, then cut out slightly larger. The smaller the window, the more designs you can make. You could also add embroidery, beads and sequins to designs.

Mount silk in centre window of 3-fold card, using double-sided tape. Stick down left-hand portion of card over back of silk.

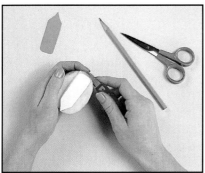

Potato cuts make quick but 'impressionistic' prints. Choose a medium-sized potato to fit comfortably into your hand. Cut in half and lay on it a motif cut from a piece of paper. Cut along edge of image, then slice potato away all round shape so that image is raised. Dry on a paper towel.

A water-based, poster or even fabric paint can be used. Apply paint to potato image, turn over and press gently but firmly onto card. Clean off paint with tissue when you want to change colour and continue, making sure overlapping colours are dry.

Some cards will be better than others, but this is part of their charm. Finish off candle card with gold pen flame and 'surround'. We have also made some cards using eraser lips and hearts — appropriate for a Valentine party.

These are special hand-made invitations for those select occasions when you want to set just the right mood in advance: a midsummer or New year party for a few intimate friends; a large family celebration lunch or dinner; a children's birthday party. For the latter, the young hosts will have much fun making the invitations themselves. An attractive invitation is the first step towards a happy and successful event. Our first invitation will contribute in a very practical way towards the evening's entertainment — a mask to wear! With the addition of full fancy dress, much fun will be derived from guessing the identity of the guests.

The mask is double, so that a couple could wear one each, perhaps decorating the plain one themselves. Trace out template *54* and cut a piece of black card 43 by 10cm (17 by 4in), score and fold 21.5cm (8½in). Transfer mask design onto black card and cut out with sharp craft knife through both thicknesses. Mark punch holes.

Collect together sequins, beads and feathers. Stick them in place with rubber-based glue. Each mask could be different. If you have bought a bag of 'sweepings' you will have a variety of sequin shapes to use. You could also add silver or gold pen designs, scraps of foil, glitter, ribbon cut into shapes — have fun!

Punch holes at either side and thread ribbon through front mask. The ribbon should be long and curled by running over scissor blades. It can be re-curled if it flattens in the post. Write your invitation message in gold or silver pen to show up on black card.

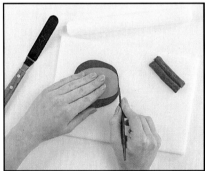

Cut pink glossy card 15 by 22cm (6 by 8½in), score and fold 11cm (4¼in). Draw out cake shape onto thin card and cut out to make template. Warm a ball of Fimo modelling material in your hands and roll out until thin. Place template on clay and cut round with a knife. Make a little dent in top centre where candle will fix.

Carefully transfer to baking foil with a spatula or knife. Bake cake according to manufacturer's instructions. Cake may stretch, but you can trim with scissors after baking. Glue doiley tablecloth on card. Cut spotted ribbon and fold around base of cake. Attach with double-sided tape or glue and add second ribbon trim.

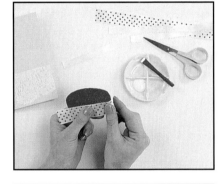

Wipe back of cake with lighter fuel to remove any grease. Dab rubber-based glue on back of cake and wait until tacky before fixing to card. Spread a fine line of glue along candle and apply to card. Hold in place for a minute or two until glue dries.

Capture the hosts of the party on a roll of film to make personal invitation cards, each one a little different. The children were delighted to be involved, especially when they opened the 'presents', even though these were empty boxes! Set up props before children come into room. Work fast before they lose concentration. A few small sweets help keep them going.

Make a mask to fit the 'sunken plate' area of the card mount and mark corners of photographs with a compass or sharp pencil point. Cut photograph with a sharp craft knife and ruler and use spray glue to affix.

Invitations can be hand-made by children too — a great way to keep them happy and involved in party planning. This rabbit is for an Easter football party given by a nine year-old boy. He drew the picture, then photocopied it a number of times. Each invitation can be hand-coloured before being glued to cards.

GIFT TAGS

Gift tags are tiny cards which can be as simple or elaborate as you you care to make them. They can reflect the contents of the gift parcel or relate to the individual's favourite leisure interest or occupation. For example for sports people, you could attach sporting postage stamps to small pieces of card and 'pink' the edges to resemble the stamp. A star sequin and a line of silver snow evokes Christmas. 'Stickers' from toy shops will give you lots of ideas. Cut out a variety of letters of the alphabet from magazines or newspapers and assemble on card to make names, or cut out an initial letter from the card to let light show through. Here are some specific ideas.

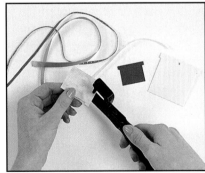

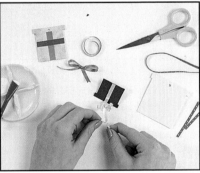

These effective tags are a useful way of using up scraps of card left over from larger projects. Cut a piece of card 10 by 5cm (4 by 2in), score and fold 5cm (2in). Measure 6mm (¼in) down from fold and mark 2mm (⅛in) in from sides before cutting through both thicknesses to give a 'lid' shape. Run blade along steel ruler twice for a clean edge.

Punch a hole through both thicknesses at centre top. Glue on ribbons. Use a bow on one, slit and curled gift-tie ribbon on another; make each tag individual. The tags can be made up in any size or colour with contrasting ribbons.

Score and fold a rectangle of thin card. Draw shape of a bow-tie on card and cut through both thicknesses. Cut a rectangle of lurex fabric slightly larger than bow and a thin strip to wrap around centre. Gather bow and hold in place with centre strip, fixing it with glue on back.

Trim edges of lurex to size of card, arrange gathers and attach to card with a dab of glue. Write your message in gold pen so that it will show up and match fabric.

Elegant and stylish tags add an extra-special touch to gift parcels. Score and fold in half a piece of white card. Draw a tie shape and cut through both thicknesses. Glue on a piece of striped wrapping paper with stripes running diagonally across card. Trim and punch a hole if needed or slip back of card behind ribbon around parcel.

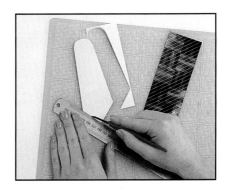

The spectrum gift tag uses origami paper. Cut a piece of white card 15 by 7.5cm (6 by 3in), score and fold 7.5cm (3in). Draw a 7.5cm (3in) square on paper, draw a line diagonally from bottom left to top right-hand corner. Draw four more at 2.5cm (1in) intervals from bottom left-hand corner to meet top and right-hand edges. Number sections.

Cut up sections and use as templates. Lay them on origami paper, one to each colour of the spectrum, and cut out. Glue paper strips to card starting from the centre. Punch a hole in the back of card and thread with gift tie-ribbon, if you wish.

Trace out template 3 and transfer design onto silver card. Cut out with scissors. You may need to burnish edges of silver card with back of your thumbnail if they have become rough. Punch a hole at top of heel and thread some silver ribbon to tie in a bow.

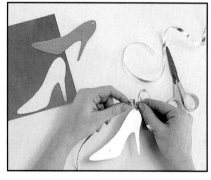

This dotty Christmas cracker can be traced from template 55 and transferred to brightly-coloured card. Cut out, fold down centre and score. Use pinking shears to trim ends of cracker. Cut three strips of florist's ribbon to fit across cracker. Pink edges, spray glue and attach to cracker. Trim excess ribbon.

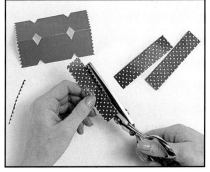

Tie two pieces of gift-wrap ribbon around 'ends' of cracker, as shown. Split ribbon down centre and curl each length.

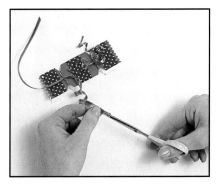

Cut a card 15 by 7.5cm (6 by 3in), score and fold 7.5cm (3in). Cut a piece of sequin waste to fit and attach to card with spray glue. Colour in circles with felt-tipped pens. Many different patterns can be made. Punch a hole in back and thread with ribbon, if desired.

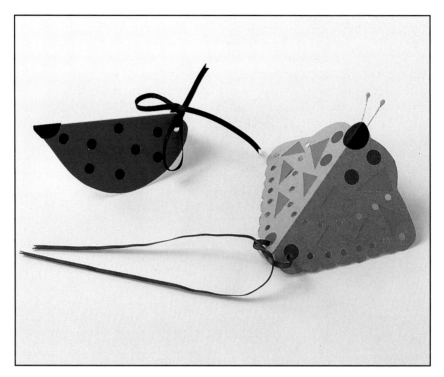

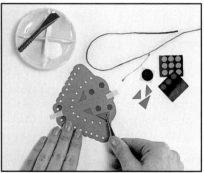

Trace out template *2* and transfer onto thin card. Place template on card, draw round and cut out. Score and fold along centre. Punch two lines of holes along wings.

Hold butterfly firmly on table with masking tape. With children's stick-on play shapes and stationers' dots, make a pattern on wings. Stick on a large dot for a head and flower stamens, coloured with felt-tipped pen, for antennae. Thread a piece of narrow satin or gift-wrap ribbon through holes in wings to attach to a parcel.

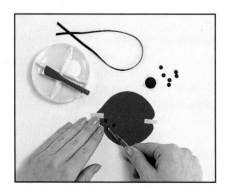

Trace out template *1* and transfer onto card. Cut out and score along centre. Hold ladybird flat on table using masking tape. Use black spots, either punched from black paper, sequins, or stationers' dots coloured with black felt-tipped pen. Glue dots randomly. Punch a hole at top of ladybird's wings and thread through narrow black satin ribbon to make a bow.

To use templates you will need either tracing, greaseproof or layout paper. Place paper over design and hold in place with small pieces of masking tape. Using a sharp, hard pencil carefully trace outline. Remove tracing and turn over. Rub over the back of the outline with a soft pencil. Turn over tracing, hold in place with masking tape and draw over outline once again with a hard pencil to transfer your image onto template card or paper. Use a ruler for straight lines. Bold dashed lines indicate that only half the template is shown (except where otherwise instructed in text). Draw half then reverse tracing. Carefully re-align and draw other half. Label right side of templates. It is best to place templates on the wrong side of fabric so that pencil lines do not show on the front — you must place them face down.

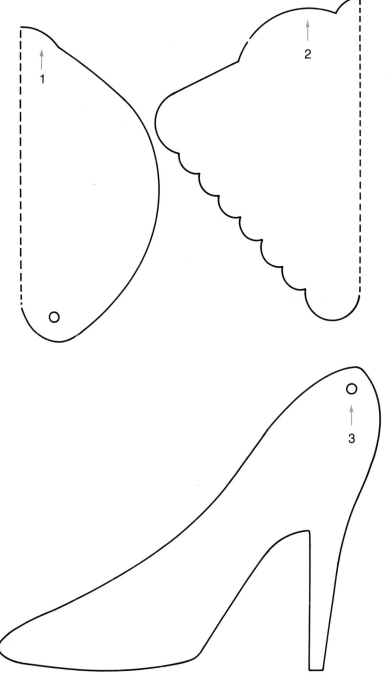

4

5

6

7

8

9

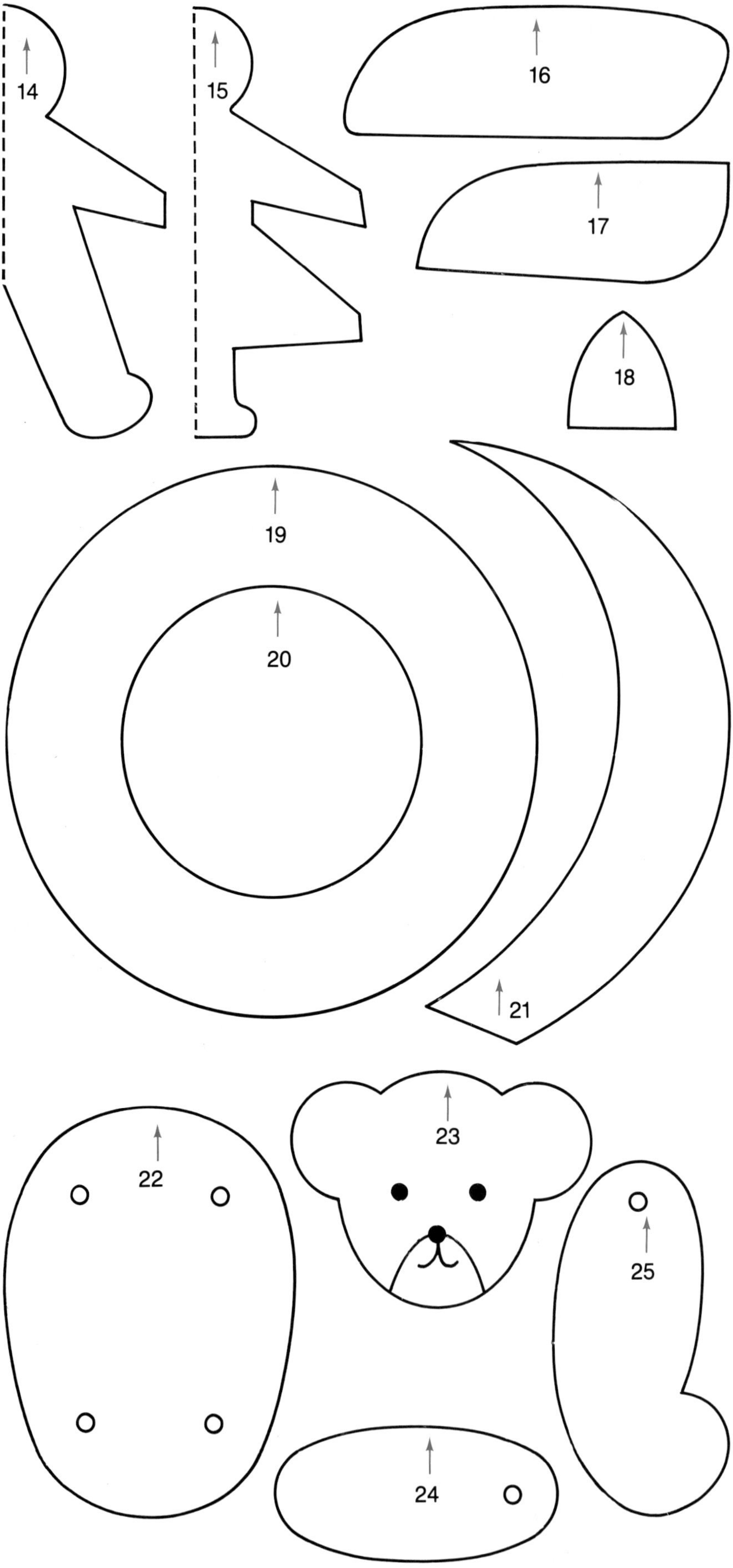

14

15

16

17

18

19

20

21

22

23

24

25

26

28

27

29

30

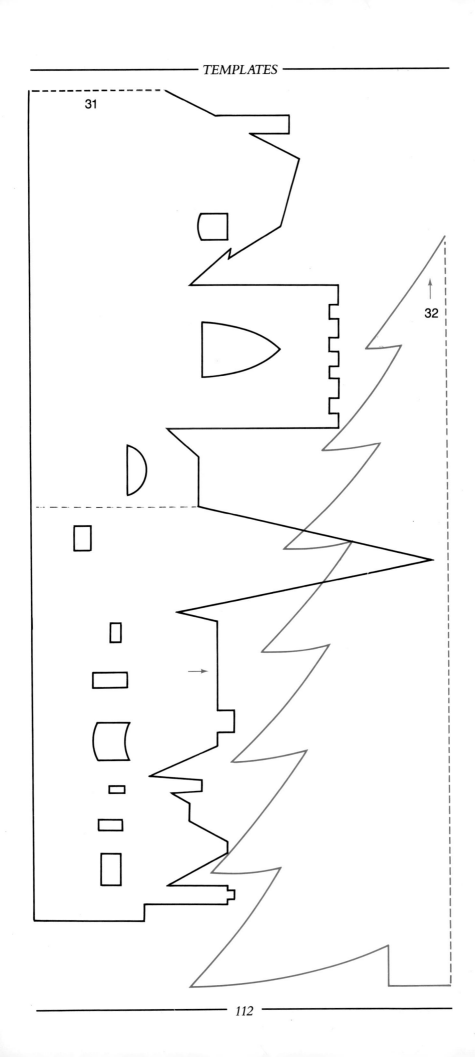

31

32

33

34

35

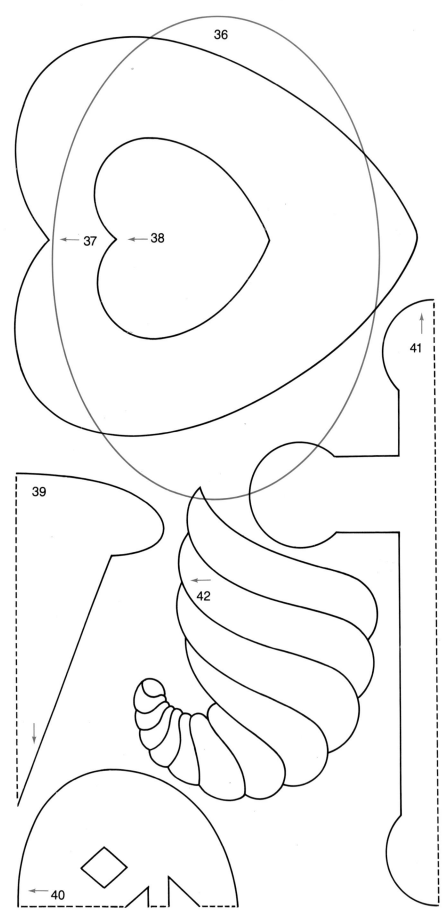

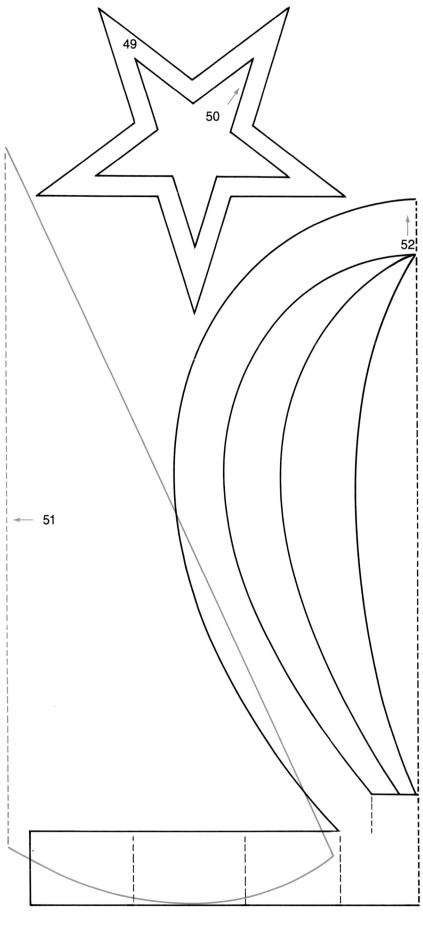

49

50

51

52

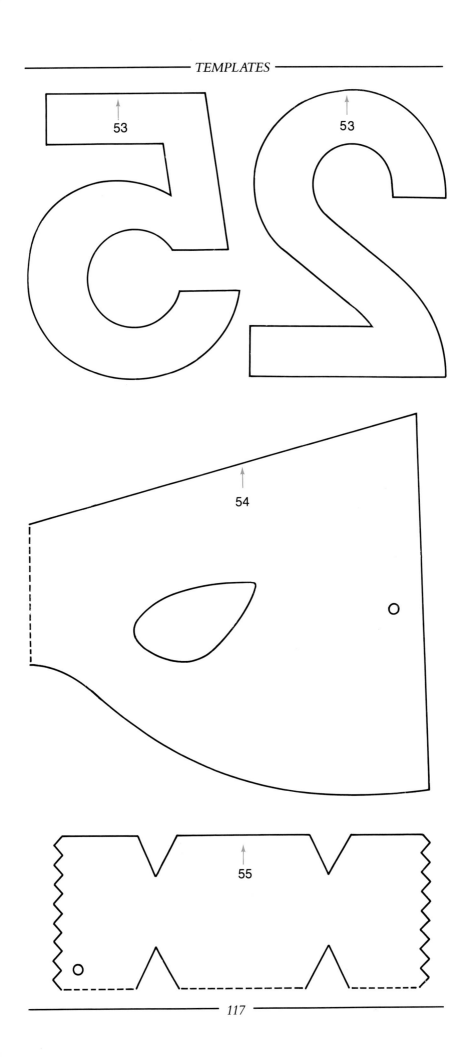

Needlepoint in Lilac (page 36)

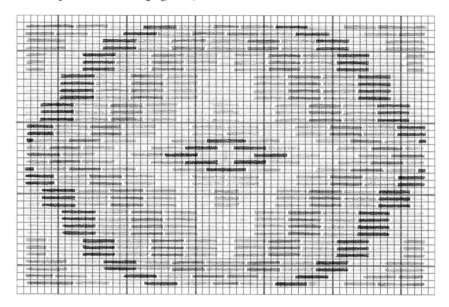

A Warm New Home Welcome (page 84)